REVISED EDITION

THE
COMMON BOOK
OF
CONSCIOUSNESS

Diana Saltoon

CELESTIALARTS

Berkeley, California

Cover and text design by David Charlsen
Composition by Recorder Typesetting Network

First Printing, 1991
0   9   8   7   6   5   4   3   2   1
96   95   94   93   92   91

Library of Congress Cataloging-in-Publication Data

Saltoon, Diana.
     The common book of consciousness / Diana Saltoon ;
     introduction by Kenneth Pelletier.—Rev. ed.
          p.   cm.
     Includes bibliographical references.
     ISBN 0-89087-627-4
     1. Consciousness.   2. Change (Psychology).
3. Stress management.   4. Health.   5. Mental Health.
I. Title.
BF311.S335   1991
613—dc20   90-20464
                                                                    CIP

Contents

Preface to the Revised Edition

This book emerged from an instinctual need for change and was the result of much trial and error, as well as work toward an understanding of consciousness and the development of the four aspects of awareness. Like others before me I found expanded consciousness to be a complex and profound goal, and defining that goal demanded a simple and direct approach. Since *The Common Book of Consciousness* was first published in 1979, the New Age has produced hundreds of books and various schools of thought that have provided theoretical information. But few books or schools furnish clear, simple methods for individual practice. Even in 1990 there still seems to be no beginning, no outline, no basic path. The question remains: what can I do *for* myself, before I do something *with* myself?

Becoming a whole and centered individual comes through an integration of body, mind, spirit and space. This is best accomplished through the realization of a lifetime exercise plan, a sane diet, a practice of meditation, and a more honest lifestyle. The difficulty is *unifying* these aspects so you will experience wonder, a new security, and a greater command of the self. Hopefully, the sense of this vital unification has been amplified in this revised edition.

In the original process of this work I met many people who, knowingly or not, helped me along my way. I would like to mention a few: Jeff Longe, Ida Grylla, Ruth Layman, Arthur M. Young, Mad Bear Anderson, and Amy Schwartz who created the illustrations. This book could not have been written without the help of Antoinette A. (Dolly) Gattozzi, a wise friend as well as an editor without equal, and the editorial assistance of Anne Weinberger. I also wish to thank Sandor Burstein for his expertise on "Alice" and "Wonderland."

Portland, Oregon
1990

Introduction

Since the early 1960s women, men, and a variety of corporations and institutions have become increasingly aware of the need to develop a means of achieving and maintaining health and well-being based upon a dramatic revision of personal lifestyle. However, until *The Common Book of Consciousness* was published, no book was available that offered a practical and effective method to achieve that end. *Common Book* was not a naive renunciation of contemporary living; it was a careful reorientation of those primary aspects of lifestyle that are necessary for sane survival in an ever-questionable technological environment.

Now, two decades later, this sophisticated revision of *Common Book* is still as pertinent as ever and still provides inspiring evidence that through "flexible yet persistent effort" any concerned individual can live a lifetime of optimum health.

In updating this work, Diana Saltoon has focused particular attention on avoiding pitfalls succumbed to by many in Western culture. For instance, while discussing the simple basics of lifestyle, she deftly blends insights derived from her practice to focus upon the "insidious infection" of living on credit that has come to threaten the lifestyle of the nation as well as the individual.

Throughout the book, well-being is viewed as the end result of combining many factors including exercise (for both cardiovascular toning as well as relaxation), diet and nutrition (including food preparation, which is too frequently overlooked) and meditation, which serves as the primary means of unifying all the practices conducive to a healthy, positive lifestyle. *Common Book* realistically emphasizes that no combination of diet, exercise or meditation is a panacea. Its theme is that optimum health can be achieved only through unifying these practices in a "systematic, slow, and thoughtful" manner. The chapters are not intended to be didactic, but rather serve as guidelines to inspire personal investigation and encourage realistic assessment of individual requirements. This point cannot be emphasized enough; since there is no uniform prescription for everyone, there is no one optimum lifestyle. There are only certain means to awaken individual awareness, to realize a "compassion for other people, other forms of life, and for all living things. And the patience that arises from trusting in this path of wonder and change." While this ideal might seem far removed from our daily activity, it is an end that can be attained.

In Chapter Two, "Exercise and the Body," the clear instructions and illustrations are enriched by Ms. Saltoon's personal experiences which lend a great deal of support to anyone who seeks significant change. Each exercise has been uniquely adapted from a yoga posture with the addition of some elements of aerobics. This sensible synthesis is characteristic of the entire book, which is never extreme in its guidelines since the thrust is to develop a style of exercise that can be practiced at any age.

There is a clear imperative for awakening to certain insights concerning diet rather than mechanically adhering to prescribed diets that are too often unhealthy. At the outset Ms. Saltoon urges us to "eliminate the promise of dieting, of eating a certain way for a certain period of time before returning to habits of consumption that caused trouble in the first place." She not only reminds us of the folly of "Yoyo-ing the body back and forth to the tune of the dietary experts," but wisely points out that "there should only be one diet. A final, lifetime diet."

Finally, she gives extensive consideration to the benefits of meditation as a complement to the physical health which has been achieved through nutrition and exercise.

Meditation is a complex matter fraught with dead ends, but in *Common Book* it is rendered with superb clarity both in terms of the underlying philosophy and the specific postures and practices described. As to the eternal question of "why meditate," Ms. Saltoon observes that in a stress-filled society "objective conditioning of the rational mind is necessary for survival." In the material world, "merely to survive is not to live a fully human life! There is no mystery to materialism, but there is to human existence. Meditation illuminates the mystery and reveals the enigma." Artfully, and in a down-to-earth manner, the subject of meditation is treated without mystification, incense, robes, or a need for the mandatory master. Meditation is seen as an inner, personal experience, a sanctity inherently devoid of any trappings, a wise removal that today can be, and frequently is, practiced in the corporate boardroom as well as the isolated retreat. The purpose is always the same: "to know who you are and how you can best change." The answers to such questions are possible, and, once known, serve as a unifying principle which binds together the separate aspects of a lifestyle of true fulfillment. This is the clarity and wisdom necessary for a fundamental reorientation of our lives: a guide in which all of the observations are well researched, succinctly stated and followed by a range of specific means from the consideration of seasonings and food preparation to the complex issue of "periodic fasting," from media as well as food.

As I pointed out in 1979, it seems appropriate that Diana Saltoon would quote from *Alice in Wonderland* since she has succeeded in presenting complex material concerning optimum health with great clarity and through personal observation and practice. Like *Alice*, *Common Book* is a work of superb logic and classical commentary by a woman who truly lives her philosophy while remaining in the mainstream of a demanding "Western" lifestyle. Although pleasantly personal, *Common Book* reflects many resources including C.J. Jung, the Nobel Prize winner Roger Sperry, Andrew Weil, Karlfried Durkheim, as well as the philosopher Huston Smith. Its insights are substantiated and honed into principles applicable to anyone seeking a more fulfilling existence; its wisdom is accessible to those who have questioned the meaning of personal existence. Living her message of transformation through her work, Diana Saltoon has found the means to convey this "systematic framework" to everyone who seeks to "meet an inner demand for a more complete and fulfilling life."

In my clinical practice and research I am constantly asked to formulate such an approach. Now it is possible to recommend a marvelous tangible resource: the revised edition of *The Common Book of Consciousness*.

Kenneth R. Pelletier
Danville, California
October, 1990

1.

Intentions

"Would you tell me, please, which way I ought to go from here?"
"That depends a good deal on where you want to get to . . . "
Lewis Carroll
Alice in Wonderland

My aim in writing *The Common Book of Consciousness* was to create an integrated and practical system that would help the concerned individual to develop greater awareness and levels of higher understanding. Through awareness we are capable of more knowledgeable responses to life and gain new appreciation of the world in which we live, both inside and outside of our skins. Using this system, awareness is developed through a combination of exercise, control of consumption, relief from stress through meditation, and the gradual alteration of lifestyle.

The Common Book of Consciousness was written for those who seek true change, who accept the necessity of lifetime exercise, and who see the gradual suicide that comes with careless eating habits. It is for those who recognize the pervasive, insidious dangers of stress and understand the need for true relaxation of body and mind. It is for those who desire to cultivate their spiritual nature and confront the need to alter the context of their lives, the places in which they live and work, in order to promote healthful change and continue the process of new growth.

I believe that increasing awareness in the four quarters of daily life—body, mind, spirit and the space in which you live and work—leads naturally to a higher understanding of the meaning of life. As your personal consciousness becomes harmoniously integrated you discover it to be far greater than the sum of its parts, for it connects you with the cosmic consciousness that animates all the things that participate in the living world. However, the immediate and practical reward for developing awareness in these four aspects is that you become physically, mentally, and emotionally healthier, more centered, stable and sound, yet more flexible and adaptable to the potential of life. You become more alive and live a better life. I see these aspects as the principal landmarks in the domain of consciousness. By developing awareness of body, mind and spirit, and by cultivating a total harmonious ecology of the self, we honor consciousness within ourselves and the world around us. In doing this we begin to live a fuller life.

This book attempts to sort out the widespread but often indiscriminate interest in health, diet, meditation, relief from stress, and the endless strategies for self-improvement. It seeks to demonstrate the correlations among these interests and the importance of increasing individual awareness, inner understanding and self-actualization. One of the most vital points to grasp is that the four aspects of daily life are inseparable. To be cognizant of the need for physical health yet ignore the benefits of meditation is an approach ultimately doomed to failure. Similarly, it is shortsighted and futile to practice meditation regularly, yet neglect the environment of your home and workplace. Developing awareness in any one, two, or even three aspects will bring positive results, but they will be short-lived fragments of what you can attain through the integration of all four.

The key to using *The Common Book of Consciousness* successfully is to recognize that seamless unity of consciousness and the consequent necessity of dealing with your self and your life *as a whole*. Today, this still sounds simplistic, if not idealistic, but it is certainly not beyond anyone willing to learn and practice. This book is designed to help you define, refine, and eventually achieve your goals. It offers a *systematic* framework for seeing and changing the way you live as you instinctively strive to meet an inner demand for a more complete and fulfilling life: a life lived with imagination and wonder, a life that allows you to know yourself and to fulfill your ultimate potential. A life blessed with joy and long moments spent in the harmony and flow of grander realities.

The past two decades have been historic in raising a vital concern with awareness and consciousness. On every level this concern has brought together psychologists, physicians, the clergy and scientists, as well as the philosophers, humanists, healers, and those who study the occult and mystery. The interrelationship between the world of the mind and spirit and the physical and natural universe is now more widely understood, and such understanding has had profound implications for individual and social transformation.

As far back as 1978, George Gallup reported that one of the most remarkable trends in the 1970s was the rising interest "in the inner, or spiritual, life." At that time, Gallup found that a projected fifty-six million Americans were involved in various religious disciplines and movements. Since then, mindfulness has become a household word, and the realization of moment-to-moment awareness—the power of "being here now"—has become common to religious recognition. In addition, rising academic attention and wide-ranging experimentation have aroused millions more to examine their own lives with a view toward expanding and heightening their consciousness. But despite the avalanche of books and articles and the far-flung operations of the New-Age consciousness-raising industry, there has been a regrettable failure to refine those aspects of awareness that are of immediate concern to common, ordinary life and to lay out the basic information needed for personal transformation.

This book is an attempt to do just that. It is designed as a primer for those who want to reorganize their time and modify their everyday activities to enhance the quality of living.

Today the concern with improving physical condition and spirituality is obvious in the emphasis on peak performance and the burgeoning popularity of exercise and meditation. The increasing interest in what one should and should not eat has become a form of obsession. This is evidence of a healthy impulse in our society toward the understanding of human potential. It is part of a worldwide trend that in coming decades will dramatically improve the quality of life and aging.

However, the interest is not limited to individual concern with exercise, diet and renewed spirituality. It extends to broader areas. Government and business have come to recognize that old ways are not working. Indeed, agencies and corporations have led the fight against debilitating lifestyle, and have been instrumental in recognizing that what was required was not only a revision of habits but new patterns of thinking—a different mindset—and, above all, individual responsibility.

To avoid smoking, to be fit, to be trim and abstain from the excessive use of alcohol and drugs of any kind is not only patriotic but a professional and social asset. An extension of these healthy practices is to replace the prevailing ethic of expensive self-indulgence with the wise conservation of global resources and the constructive application of human potential. One of the accomplishments of the New Age movement has been the realization that the health of the planet is as important as that of the individual, and the greater realization that they are one and the same.

These changes in awareness serve to illustrate that tremendous forces are coming to bear on us *simultaneously*, and that tens of millions of world citizens are moving into processes of personal change which add up to sweeping changes in the global society. However, what should never be ignored is the fact that at the center of this often misunderstood "consciousness movement" are you and your own instinct to develop greater awareness and the desire to rid your life of self-imposed tyrannies: destructive or futile habits of body and mind, spiritual stagnation, and negative lifestyle. These are all parts of a whole, and the whole is you. Dabbling in or even devotedly concentrating on one or a few of the parts can be moves in the right direction if they provide a vision of the wholeness that totally supports your life. However vague or fleeting, that vision will inspire you—as it did me—to take on the whole challenge of reaching your human potential.

To achieve this goal, a *unified* program for the development of awareness is imperative. It is not enough just to "get more exercise" or "cut down" on eating. "Getting away from it all" can actually increase stress levels if done without knowing the fundamentals of true relaxation. Spending a "little more time on yourself" can be lonely and pointless unless you have created an atmosphere conducive to a scheme of personal growth, a place in which you can practice a complete ecology of the self. Only to the extent that you have the courage and the sincerity of purpose to stride toward wholeness will you fully satisfy the soundest instinct of your life.

The Common Book of Consciousness is not exhaustive, nor is it meant to be definitive. It reflects a seasoned and personal point of view. It is a guide, a reference book for a basic system of life practices, designed to help develop awareness and expand consciousness. The particulars can be tailored to your individual needs. What we do determines the quality of our lives, and I believe that we are destined to refine our lives so that "something more" will arise in our awareness.

For me, it all began nearly twenty-six years ago when I lived in New York City and, through curiosity and chance, was introduced to yoga. I will never forget meeting my first teacher of hatha yoga. Ida was nearly sixty yet she glowed with health and vitality. Her physical poise and posture were those of a much younger woman; certainly her agility exceeded my own in gracefulness and strength.

I was intrigued. If yoga could produce such energy and prevent the usual deleterious effects of aging then it was for me! It was not just Ida's surface aspect of a vividly healthful appearance, it was her total presence. There was a relaxed alertness, an alive patience, a tolerance blended with warmth and compassion that endeared her to me. I longed to be able to live as gracefully as she did.

Back then it took several years to discover that exercise in itself (what I learned as the hatha limb of the classical eight-limbed yoga) would change nothing. Doing yogic exercises certainly made my body more limber. Afterwards I felt relaxed and, for a short while, energized. But, by returning to old habits and hectic schedules, I did not experience any dramatic differences. Yogic exercise was a magnificent discipline but, by itself, did not induce the change I had hoped would come. It caused me to become newly aware of my body but it did not alter the total sense of my life. Nevertheless, yoga was the first step toward my realization that I needed more—and less.

I say less because it gradually dawned on me that, like almost everyone else, I often ate and drank too much and consumed items of little or no nutritional value. Eventually exercise, the first line of body awareness, led to a careful consideration of eating habits and the discovery that exercise and consumption are highly interactive. I came to see that what I consumed, both in food and in the external impressions I took in deliberately (or was exposed to willy-nilly by the circumstances of daily life), greatly affected me both physically and mentally. As my awareness of this connection increased and I began to modify my life practices, my spiritual dimension came increasingly into focus as a vital part of my whole being. Learning to tend and cultivate this aspect of life through some kind of meditative removal seemed to lie at the very heart of my yearning for wholeness and fulfillment. Lastly I realized that awareness and refinement of my inner spaces of body, mind and spirit required control of my outer environment, the spaces in which I lived my daily life, the elements that comprised my lifestyle.

These learning experiences took place over the course of many years. It was often a confusing time during which I realized I had become a student of consciousness. At that time, in the late 1960s and early 1970s, I had considered myself a woman leading a different life, hardly typical of my time. I had always been "a working woman" and had, as it happened, a rewarding career as an international flight attendant. However, constant travel to foreign cities had gradually begun to illuminate the gross failings of my American diet. That diet, combined with the strain of jet lag, eventually produced serious physical consequences that had to be dealt with. Having neither the inspiration nor the time for deep study and research, I simply learned what I could from eclectic reading and trusted my intuition to guide me forward at a pace commensurate with my needs. At the time I believed that was the right and proper route, and I know now that it was effective.

The subject of yoga is wide and deep. According to the Sanskrit scholar Jean Varenne, the word "yoga" should be understood as meaning "magic recipe," or "method." Certainly the yogic recipe is of great complexity and subtlety. In looking to it for direction and clues on how to define and proceed toward my goals, I was very impressed but also put off. It seemed extreme: too specific and almost contradictory to what I was and how I wished to live. I wanted to improve my life through change but not to alter it radically. I did not want to withdraw. I admired the philosophy of yoga but found the severity of its discipline to be impractical and limited.

I carried on with the exercises and gradually adapted and shaped them into the sets and series that produced the maximum beneficial effects for me. The second chapter of this book outlines the program I devised and still follow. The movements are primarily based on hatha yoga exercises and the program is designed to serve you for a lifetime. I believe that you should exercise with a lifelong aim of maintaining health and preventing the needless debilities that too often accompany aging. This program rejects excessive athleticism. Unless you are a highly competitive athlete, developing extreme muscularity is pointless.

In Chapter Three I have tried to refine a final, lifetime diet designed to eliminate the *traditional* means of diet control, which are not only impractical but actually destructive to anyone intent upon living a full life. There are no more than a dozen simple principles concerning what and how much to eat in order to get the nutrition and energy that you need. These are presented along with pointers on cooking and meal planning, as well as on fasting. In addition to what you eat, your daily diet consists of all your practices involving food. A primary aim of the lifetime diet is to bring you back to the sources of food, inspiring you to feel and see the preparation and consumption of food as a vital part of body-mind awareness.

Regular exercise and a radically revised diet lead naturally to an active concern about stress, for stress-related psychosomatic disorders have reached almost epidemic proportions. Today we have come to see that stress that becomes *distress* is one of the most pervasive fatal factors of our time. It is an indirect and, in many cases, a direct contributor to car accidents and acts of social violence, as well as to the cancers, heart attacks, ulcers, respiratory ailments and other diseases which plague the middle and later years of human beings.

Chapter Four deals with meditation, the *key* to profoundly restorative relaxation. A daily habit of meditation (or some form of meditative removal) is not only an excellent antidote to stress, but it brings us in contact with that essential sense of the self that, sadly, we seem to have lost.

Lifestyle is the area of concern covered in Chapter Five, which discusses the possibilities for creating a fruitful private life and escaping the trap of materialism and ambiguous and often duplicitous authoritarianism. If the "New Age" has taught anything, it is that it is foolhardy for anyone to attempt drastic or abrupt changes in lifestyle. After too many years of painful and sometimes hilarious or embarrassing experiences, I can vouch for the great importance of changing your lifestyle with subtlety.

To improve health we can exercise and change our eating habits. To relax and gain great psychic and psychological centeredness we can meditate. These practices produce immediate and direct effects. But there are no prescriptions for changing lifestyle. Instead, it simply happens more or less as follows: the practices related to exercise, consumption, and meditation, become a process of unification through which lifestyle begins to change. Attitudes and practices are the foundation for change. Next, the home and workplace are seen as total environments which must be critically appraised and appropriately altered. Lastly, our interactions with society and its institutions require tougher consideration. These are the elements that determine the quality of private life, and it is within private life that awareness is best developed. This chapter suggests ways in which you can not only support and foster the three basic activities of daily awareness—exercise, consumption, and meditation—but refine the styles of inner attitudes and outer environments that dominate the way you live moment-to-moment.

Awareness of lifestyle is no less vital to consciousness than are physical fitness, proper nutrition and psycho-spiritual centeredness. Cultivating awareness in all four aspects is the key to *The Common Book of Consciousness*.

> *The greatest decisions of human life have as a rule far more to do with the instincts and other mysterious unconscious factors than with the conscious will and well-meaning reasonableness. The shoe that fits one person pinches another; there can be no recipe for the living that suits all cases. Each of us carries his own life form—an indeterminable form which cannot be superseded by an other.*
>
> Carl Gustav Jung

The dynamics of a unified practice of awareness are powerful. They entail physical, psychic, and social consequences that are of incalculable benefit to the person who follows them. Yet such a practice is not as narcissistic or selfish as some claim. I believe that goodness proceeds from within as surely as it flows from without. Trite but true, it is still rightly said that charity begins at home—so too with understanding and love of the self. We are responsible for ourselves and should fulfill that task in the most intelligent and deeply caring way. I think that the phenomenal interest in awareness and consciousness comes from an instinctual recognition on the part of every concerned individual that there is something more, something better for each one of us. It is a recognition that brings hope for our collective future.

There is no reason to continue to plod through old patterns or suffer from dated habits. The historian Theodore Roszak has written that "we desperately need to outgrow the dismal and diminished human image we inherit from the past two centuries of industrialism. We need a radically altered conception of ourselves, our primary needs, of our place in nature. . . . "

We grow from within, and it is in our human potential to know ourselves and to believe in our evolution. It has become painfully obvious that the society in which we live does not cherish individual lives. The authorities that control it are far more invested in reaping the benefits of the technological and materialistic jungle in which all of us are ensnared. The practice of unified awareness provides a path through that jungle, a means whereby you, the individual, regain command of your life.

Charges of narcissism and cynical criticism of a "me generation," of a politically uncaring elite, still sound like a pessimistic Victorian crone taking to task the New Age individual—mourning the loss of dated manners and mores and condemning "degrading hedonism." The strong prejudice against trying for new solutions often uses ridicule, and frequently is politically or economically motivated. Whatever the complicated case may be, I have found most warnings absurd. I have been able to exercise and meditate regularly, stay well nourished on a modest budget, and define my needs and priorities without losing my allegiances to community and country or sacrificing the quality of my personal relationships. I accomplished all of this without dropping out in any sense, without escaping those family, social, and political duties that may face any woman or man.

According to Tarthang Tulku, a contemporary Master of Tibetan Buddhism, "We can be 'selfish' in taking care of ourselves . . . by making our minds and bodies as harmonized as possible." At the same time you come to accept and appreciate yourself, you become open to compassion for others. He writes, "Through the integration and balancing of our minds and bodies, it is possible to attain the inner peace and joy which is love itself." Love is the ultimate flower of living consciousness, and to live in love and to become love is to merge with your spirit. You travel a circle but always come back to this core of yourself. It is a journey that merges with wisdom and understanding. By living consciousness we open ourselves to love, the genius of our species. We open our own doors of perception and develop the intuitive and psychic abilities that are part of our heritage. We go beyond the development of psychic power toward a deeper understanding of human suffering and delusion. These perceptions strengthen our core with trust and further expand our consciousness. As the mystery reveals itself we see we are each a single thread woven into a cosmic pattern that is beyond intellectual comprehension or verbal expression. To gaze is to see but a segment. The pattern extends into never-ending cycles of creation and degeneration. Through awareness we spin our own thread and knowingly participate in a mandala of life. We free the spirit and let it soar. With love as a companion we are invincible.

The lives most of us lead are contained and conditioned. Freedom comes from allowing our spirit to soar freely. All of us are endowed with this noblest of intentions. To carry it out, however, requires developing awareness and taking control of our lives. "We learn by doing!" says a Jonathan Winters character at the end of a painful but particularly droll routine. Our predicaments are often deeply confounding, but we must not take things too seriously, nor doubt that we are smart enough to meet the requirements. Much of what is called learning is a kind of rediscovery of things already known though long forgotten. Once you have begun a unified practice of awareness you will know how to proceed toward final goals, and you will have the means to get there. Whether you tarry to seek past lives, to see death for what it is, or to find a guru is up to you, of course. I urge you to stay focused on everyday, ordinary problems throughout any search.

The guidelines offered in *The Common Book of Consciousness* are simple in conception and straightforward in presentation. Few of you will be unfamiliar with the elements offered here; some might consider them simplistic. Certainly the points developed in this book are intellectually simple. A line I once read summing up a harrowing adventure novel by Lionel Davidson strikes me as being relevant: "If experience taught anything it was not to think too much, but to sharpen up the responses." Many waste time thinking about their dwindling vitality, stale routines, sterile pursuits, and the superficiality of their lives. To wrestle abstractly with complex propositions and large philosophical issues will exercise the intellect, but it will not change life. The purpose of this book is to help you choose areas of your life that could benefit from change, make those changes, and thereby develop your own diversity. The object is to show a unified means for personal exploration, growth and transcendence.

L*ive in each season as it passes; breathe the air; drink the drink; taste the fruit and resign yourself to the influence of each. Let them be your only diet, drink and botanical medicines. Be blown on by all the winds. Open all your pores and bathe in all the tides of nature, in all her streams and oceans, at all seasons.*

Henry David Thoreau

Various fashions have been attached to the development of awareness, however one aspect that has always been emphasized is the naturalness of this endeavor, as put so eloquently by Thoreau. I disagree with those who feel it is necessary to seek quietude by dropping out of society in order to achieve expanded consciousness. For the majority of these people such a course is fraught with confusion and can end in overwhelming disappointment. We have all suffered one or more of the antisocial, burn-out cases. We know the effects, the regrets. To drop out by surrendering to religious extremism or foolish drug use, even moving to a utopian commune—to name but a few of the most notorious instances—can provoke psychological and cultural shocks that distort awareness rather than enhance it.

Awareness is as natural to the human condition as breathing. Awareness can be developed virtually any place at any time by anyone of any age. Urban, suburban, or country settings are equally adequate. In the beginning no special expertise need be sought. No special group or religion is mandatory. After developing a habit of regular exercise and learning to control consumption, after forming a solid meditative habit and coordinating this with your own command of silence and privacy, freedom and spirituality will come in the form you need. Too often the practical elicitation of one's spiritual nature is thought to be dependent upon a religious inspiration or discipline. This is not necessarily so. By unifying the tangible activities of awareness you bring together mind and body and prepare yourself for spiritual awakening and growth that will enhance religious choice.

Being natural and utterly immediate, the practice of awareness does not exclude any aspect of life nor neglect historical continuity. Yogi Sujit has stated, "Cosmic consciousness is worthless without social consciousness . . . we must recharge our energies to go back to the battlefield of life, not escape." Yogi Vishnu Devananda reminds us, "Many are working today for the promotion of world peace without first having peace within themselves. How can the blind help the blind? This world can be saved only by those who have already saved themselves." In short, those who make accusations of narcissism fail to see that individual psychosomatic/psycho-spiritual unity is one source of beneficial social change.

Nor is this practice easy despite its ordinariness. There is no glamour in unifying the four quarters of consciousness. To develop awareness and fulfill one's human potential requires sincerity, patience and hard work.

We look to the earth and sift the sands in the hope of uncovering some clue that might throw light on the origin and purpose of our existence. We look to the heavens for deliverance. By looking inward—directing effort toward increasing awareness—we can find what we seek within the self.

Students of consciousness, those some also call spiritual explorers, have appeared regularly throughout history. The practice of unifying awareness and enlarging personal consciousness with the goal of transcendence is humankind's Primordial Tradition, to use the designation given it by the historian Huston Smith. In the past, the overwhelming majority of these individuals led lives as common and ordinary as you and I do. A few of them—poets, scholars, spiritual masters, thinkers and artists—have left records of their experiences that we can use in our studies. (No committee wrote *The Bhagavad Gita* or fashioned the formula $E = mc^2$). One by one, we gladly join them on the bedrock of reality, and we find many others there similarly occupied. They are related to us in countless ways but basically they are co-teachers and co-students. We are all engaged in the same noble task.

To go beyond the ordinary realms of expectation we must be willing to explore the *terra incognita*—the unknown country—of the mind. Extrasensory perception, psychic healing and other phenomena are but a part of what exists within the mind, but these will not concern us here. In the 1980s scientists learned a great deal about the brain and nervous system, but this too is excluded from consideration here because science is just beginning to recognize that the mind is not a by-product of the brain. In the early 1970s the psychologist Robert Ornstein admitted that academic psychology had for the past seventy years refused to study the essential questions of its discipline. These questions were, he wrote in the preface to *The Nature of Human Consciousness*: "How does the mind work? What are the major dimensions of human consciousness? Is consciousness individual or cosmic? What means are there to extend human consciousness?" However, today those questions are being addressed. In 1986 the Nobel laureate Roger Sperry theorized that instead of "excluding mind and spirit, as had been the rule for all of us in brain-behavior science for many decades, my new logic required that mental and 'spiritual' forces be reinstated at the top of the brain's causal control hierarchy."

This is an historic turn and one that should inspire any program of developing awareness. Though optimistic, I try to be realistic about the many pitfalls and dead ends that may stymie the beginner. The root work of discipline and control is never easy. The results, however, can be dramatic. As awareness increases you realize that you are constantly evolving to fulfill a universal scheme of totality. To celebrate the joy of complete and total life, to realize the whole of your potential requires you to enter that inner unknown country and trustingly step into other realms of human existence far more spacious, wondrous, and drenched in reality than those to which you are accustomed. The sails are trimmed: the celebration begins when you embark.

2.

Exercise and the Body

> ... **S**elf-help is the only way open to everyone.
> The way is hard and complicated, but for every person who feels
> the need for change and improvement, it is within the limits of
> practical possibility.
>
> Moshe Feldenkrais
> *Awareness through Movement*

I.

The body comes first. A whole and healthy body is a great gift, and maintaining sound physical health is the most basic responsibility we have. So much depends upon realizing that health is a condition that can be improved and controlled. The rest of your life depends on it.

In recent years the excitement surrounding exercise and diet has become epidemic. However, considering that equal importance must be given to meditation and lifestyle, it's necessary to temper such excitement. Research has clearly shown that whether or not you enjoy a long and vigorously healthy lifetime depends primarily on how you balance daily life. Meeting the body's needs for exercise and proper nutrition is the first line of defense against the encroachment of those debilitating diseases so tragically characteristic of the middle and later decades of life. Freedom from infirmity is certainly important to the body's well-being which is, in turn, the physical frame wherein the person's psychosomatic and psycho-spiritual selves are formed. The physical and nonphysical aspects of your whole self are believed to be totally interpenetrating. Nevertheless, it makes sense

13

from the point of view of self-education to start with the most obvious, easily perceived aspect—literally, the living material of one's human organism: one's body. That is what makes exercise and diet the starting points of any effort to unify the development of awareness.

A healthy body is fit, flexible, and able to relax. Muscles are in tone; breathing and blood circulation are efficient; joints and tendons are pliable; and the stresses of everyday life are regularly relieved through meditative relaxation. Beyond this, healthy people are conscious of—and feel a sense of solidarity with—their bodies. They sense trust and cooperation between the mind and body. In this way the fundamental psychosomatic unity of human life is given positive expression. Healthy people also have a rich appreciation of personal reality. They experience the physical world as being "here and now." Yet, this feeling of solidity and substance does not have the effect of weighing them down. Quite the opposite is true.

As physical health improves and mind-body integrity increases, the quality of physical energy changes. It becomes lighter, clearer, more abundant, and somehow more intelligent. This is the expression of the psycho-spiritual aspect of human nature. In sum, the optimally healthy person is one who is functioning harmoniously in body, mind, and spirit.

Only a small fraction of all people are optimally healthy. A much larger portion are poorly developed or clearly ill and in need of medical care. Even among the great majority who have no clear health problems, there is always room for improvement. But the way for anyone to begin moving toward optimum health is to cultivate a daily habit of exercise and disciplined movement that both promotes physical health and develops body awareness. The second stage is when you realize that what you eat affects not only the health of your body but also the quality of your energy. Permanently changing your eating habits for the better is the goal of the lifetime diet presented in the following chapter. The third stage involves learning how to allow the physical body to experience deeply restorative relaxation and, beyond that, to free the spirit for exploration of whole new worlds of consciousness. The fourth and final stage deals with putting all this together into a personally satisfying lifestyle. In my experience, every stage is vital to the development of wholeness, and none is secondary or subordinate to the others.

Nevertheless, we have to start somewhere and build from there. I believe that it's best to begin with caring for the physical body. By attending to the body's need for exercise, by establishing a discipline, creating an exercise program for yourself that is efficient and enjoyable, you have begun not only to change your life but the circumstance of your death as well.

The fourteen exercises offered here have been freely adapted from yoga postures with the addition of some elements from Western-style calisthenics. They are designed to enable you to gradually bring your body into awareness while increasing its suppleness and vigor. No matter the size and shape of your body, how much or how little exercise you have done in the past, no matter what your particular physical limitations or age might be, you can devise a suitable program from the series and sets suggested. The emphasis should be on how you do each exercise rather than how many exercises you perform. Do those you most enjoy but always work on others you have not yet mastered and, above all, always challenge yourself a little bit more. Exercise should never be boring. It should never tire you; rather it should please and invigorate. Be patient in learning the details of the movements and allow yourself to enjoy what you are doing.

These exercise routines are not for the competitive athlete whose aims in general are antagonistic to those of people who wish to benefit from exercise for a longer, better life. Competitive athletes often over-develop their muscles and bodily skills in order to compete. Such training is hardly congenial to the unification and wholeness needed to support longevity.

By contrast brisk walking, swimming, jogging, bicycling and other forms of aerobic exercise are pleasurable and offer excellent benefits. They are vigorous whole-body activities that efficiently condition the cardiovascular and respiratory systems, thereby improving the heart and blood circulation. These are ideal activities for anyone interested in a meaningful and healthy life. The critical elements of an active, vibrant body are a flexible spine and a sound heart and lungs. Maintaining efficient circulation of oxygen-rich blood is the key to preventing senility.

One reason jogging has become so popular is that it requires no costly equipment or special facilities. For the same reason walking is the favorite exercise for Americans aged twenty or more according to the National Center for Health Statistics. I prefer brisk walking to jogging. Although walking in a park or woodlands is more time-consuming I find it more enjoyable, and I believe that enjoyment is the key to lifetime exercise.

There is another class of whole-body exercises that are not as widely appreciated although equally vital to health. Such exercises are generally done indoors and in private, and call for a different kind of discipline. This class of exercise calls attention to the body's need for subtle-sense, integrative activity. The need to integrate or harmoniously tune the finer levels of physical functioning is less obvious—but no less important to health and longevity—than the vigorous conditioning of the heart and lungs. The fourteen exercises presented in this chapter belong in this class of integrative exercise.

In creating your own program you should include both vigorous and integrative types of exercise. If you already jog, swim, or walk and wish to capitalize fully on these activities, you can begin by practicing the exercises offered here. Anyone can enhance his or her well-being by making these exercises part of daily life. This is easier than you might imagine, for they can be performed no matter the weather or time of day. As little as twenty minutes a day, with almost no time needed for preparation or winding down, can make a successful beginning program.

Most significantly, the exercises call for slow, careful execution and great concentration. They are ideal for people beginning on a path of unified self-knowledge, for people who not only wish to be physically fit but also want to develop greater awareness of their bodies. This is the beginning of freeing the mind-body for other awareness.

The most important advantage of following these routines is that you are working on three levels simultaneously. On one level you stretch muscles and improve flexibility and circulation; you are taking the gentle path to becoming physically fit. On the second, you are practicing body awareness, enhancing inner sensibilities, tuning into the joyful feelings of life within your skin; you are on a path leading to optimum health. On the third level you are systematically learning to relax in that each exercise calls for mild tension, with awareness of that tension, followed by brief rest. Each practice session should end with the deeply relaxing exercise traditionally called *Going Within*, which is marvelously effective for relieving stress. *Going Within* also prepares a quiet body state, a meditative stillness in which you begin to realize a center of utter calm deep inside yourself. At the third level, then, you are on a path toward spiritual freedom.

Too few people realize the crucial importance of knowing how to relax completely, right down into the bones and beyond. From the health point of view, physicians have come to agree with Elmer and Alyce Green of the Menninger Foundation who said, "It is not life that kills us; rather it is our reaction to it, and this reaction can be to a considerable extent self-chosen." Now it is common knowledge that stress that is *not* relieved through deep relaxation becomes *distress*, which leads to *dis-ease*. Deep relaxation, regularly practiced, is what we can choose as our response to the daily stress we often relish but which threatens to get the better of us if we let it tick away like a time bomb under our skin. Such potentially damaging stress can be defused by deep relaxation. You cannot do the body, or the self, a greater favor than this.

Most people tend to ignore the active role of awareness in relaxation. True relaxation requires concentration and the withdrawal of attention from daily life. Gathering attention to an inward focus and quieting the body happen together. In short, true relaxation is a body-and-mind event.

All this will become clear as you gradually learn and regularly practice the exercises in this chapter. In so doing you will make a firm commitment to changing your life, becoming and being the person you wish to be.

I would like to mention one aspect of relaxation before turning to the routines that will make up your structured program. It is a way of focusing immediate attention on breathing, which can be done anywhere at any time. In fact, I especially recommend doing it before you interact with other people—on the job; in the kitchen with the family; in the living room with friends; on a bus or in a restaurant. It takes only a moment and, because it utilizes the power of breath, it works wonders.

A BREATHER

While seated, let your gaze drop to an easy-feeling point in midspace. Then, relax your face: feel the skin of the forehead and around the eyes let go; feel the cheeks and lips relax. As you do this, take a full breath from the belly, exhale slowly, and gently straighten your posture so that your body is not twisted or slumped. Rest your hands on your lap. Keep your lips closed and breathe only through your nose. Continue to be aware of full, comfortable breathing and of your relaxed face.

The key to a relaxed face is relaxed teeth. When your bite is relaxed, your teeth are just barely apart. Gently put them in that position while you continue breathing. Relaxed teeth indicate a relaxed jaw. Now your whole head and face are momentarily relieved of the tensions brought about by social interaction. For just a moment or two, you are restored to the self. You go to the wellspring within, and carefully consider breath and breathing. Then you are free to go on or rejoin others with renewed gusto for participation, interaction and cooperation.

If you can, take another moment or so and carry on with relaxing the whole of your upper body. Starting with the feeling of that relaxed jaw, feel the neck muscles relax and let go from below the ears and under the jaw right out to the tips of each shoulder. Continue breathing from the abdomen and feel your shoulder blades, upper arms and upper chest relax. Do not sag, as this would interfere with free and full breathing which is the key to this exercise. Finally, let go of tension in your lower arms, wrists and hands. Continue abdominal breathing, always being aware of how it guides the relaxation through your body.

This exercise for practicing relaxation complements *Going Within*, and both are linked to meditation postures and practices outlined in Chapter Four. In the past ten years the idea of *Going Within* has gained popular recognition on many levels, but some people still fail to appreciate the importance of relaxed breathing. It is really so simple. Basically, one sits still and is sensitive to breath. By investing this natural function with conscious attention, one can add great power to its benefits.

Like breathing, waking is a natural act we perform automatically. Until a few years ago, we seldom considered that the act of waking from a night's sleep was subject to increased awareness and change. By the time a person has reached the age of thirty, she or he has awakened to nearly 11,000 days; by fifty, to more than 18,000. "Beginning the new day" becomes so automatic it seems absurd to consider how it is done. Yet the last moments of sleep, the transition between sleep and wakefulness, are a time of rare importance. How they are experienced influences how we live. No matter what problems are to be faced, what trials the day may bring, waking is a time for brief inward focus on the sense of that gap between the end of one state of consciousness and the beginning of another. Waking is a crucial act and should neither be overlooked nor excluded from change. The mechanics of waking are simple, but what is important is learning *why* a sympathetic procedure of waking is necessary. The answer emerges as you make changes and observe their effects. The following steps will improve your waking.

ON AWAKENING

When you wake up, you arrive. Consequently, learn to care for yourself as you emerge from sleep. Remain quiet a moment or two. If possible, it is best to train yourself to awaken naturally at a given time and dispense with the use of an alarm. The most important thing is not to be jarred from sleep or to bolt out of bed. Tune into the moment, for this is a time for positive affirmation. Breathe, stretch, and gently roll your body from side to side. On rising swing both legs to the floor and lift your weight onto both feet equally. If the details of a dream seem significant, take a moment to write them down.

Now is an ideal time for meditation. However, you may want to meditate later and exercise instead. A jog or brisk walk in the early morning clears the head and quickens the blood. It is a splendid way to begin the day, but not everyone can afford to do so. Perhaps children need to be sent to school or business calls need to be made. Countless demands can postpone exercise or meditation, but nothing should disrupt the private moments of waking. Whatever your personal responsibilities, try always to make your waking moments a time of intimate centeredness.

People still complain, "I don't have time to exercise!" Yet we have time to waste and time to see those friends who sour us or add little to our lives. We must spend time to run errands, but we often shop needlessly or indulge in trivial pursuits. Why then is it so difficult to devote thirty minutes or an hour each day to the body and mind? So little time is spent on the self that we need to ask "Who are we living for?" To live a life of awareness you must begin by accepting the responsibility of caring for the body. No one else will do it for you; no one can. To build and maintain health and purity is not vain or selfish. It is the first step in living more fully and freeing your energy so that you may better serve others. We begin by devoting time to the body, and in so doing we use our right to change what we are and seek what we want to become.

II.

Select the routines for your personal program from the fourteen exercises presented in this section. Read each one through carefully and look closely at the accompanying illustrations. As you do so, try to visualize yourself moving as indicated, step by step. Don't actually carry out the instructions at this time, but do pause during your reading and try to imagine your torso, limbs, and head moving in the prescribed ways. Moshe Feldenkrais, developer of a highly effective system of physical rehabilitation, has repeatedly demonstrated the power of visualization in his work with thousands of patients and students. Visualizing your body moving as instructed, in the absence of any contrary feedback arising from the body's current limitations, guarantees success in the psychic aspect of your psychosomatic self. True, you probably will practice many weeks before your physical body totally responds to the commands of your will. Nevertheless, it is extremely useful at the very start to see yourself in your mind's eye moving with beautiful precision and control.

Before changing or increasing your physical activity, it is always wise to check with a physician or fitness expert in order to avoid unnecessary strain or injury, as well as to immediately respond to any physical discomfort or irregularity. This is especially true when practicing yoga, a radically different approach to well-being. Extreme forms of yoga are fine for the yogi, but too demanding for Westerners who need to temper exercise according to their profession and flexibility. The attitude of the body at work needs to be considered. For example, a sedentary job where one is continually bent over a desk will cause neck and spinal stiffness that will require a gentler and more patient participation in the exercises.

THE FOURTEEN EXERCISES

1. Sun Series
2. For the Legs
3. Rocking
4. Headstand
5. Shoulderstand
6. Half Fish
7. Plow
8. Plow Combination
9. The Rise
10. For the Stomach
11. Breathing
12. For the Eyes
13. For the Neck
14. Going Within

To begin practicing these exercises you will need to reserve a half-hour in your daily schedule. It can be early morning, before or after a jog or brisk walk, right before bed, during a work break if your work place provides adequate space, or after work but before dinner. Fit in the half-hour (or more) whenever it suits you. Always begin with the *Sun Series*, then proceed to perform all the exercises, which may require two or three sessions. Or you may prefer to select seven routines you want to master first and concentrate on them for the time being. I recommend the following sequence of exercises for the beginner: *Sun Series, Leg Exercises, Rocking, Breathing, For the Eyes, Neck Exercises, Going Within*. When you have memorized the details of these exercises and practiced them for several weeks, add or substitute one or more of the remaining exercises. Keep incorporating new routines and rotating the total fourteen until, within three or four months, you have learned all of them. From this point on, the pleasure of daily practice and the dramatic mind-body improvement you experience will have made your program an integral part of your life.

Remember that seeing is believing. Believe you can make profoundly beneficial changes in your physical body, then act on this belief and you will see for yourself. As a beginner, don't be discouraged. The more difficult an exercise seems the more you can benefit from it. If you find your routine easy, hold the postures a little longer than suggested.

Whatever your condition, go easy; never strain. There is no hurry, no time frame; there are no competitive pressures. This gentle approach absolutely excludes quick, strenuous movements that might cause trouble. The key to correct performance—working slowly, carefully, and with great concentration—is facilitated by breathing fully through the nose at all times. Your pace when exercising is deliberate, never stressful, and there is never a need to take in extra oxygen through your mouth. The lips are closed and teeth relaxed as in *Taking a Breather*. As I have said before, the *why* of doing these exercises is as important as *how* you do them. Practice for your own sake, consciously choosing optimum health as your goal.

SUGGESTIONS

Dress is important to physical exercise in that what you wear can set the tone and encourage the habit of a daily routine. Whatever you choose to wear should be comfortable and allow for free movement and breathing.

Exercise in a well-ventilated room or in a private place outdoors. Never exercise on a full stomach, and wait at least a half-hour after exercising before having a meal. Practice daily if you can, or at least four times a week, keeping to the same days and hours if possible.

Sun Series

This series of twelve movements limbers you up for other exercises. I have found that these whole-body stretches make the body pliant and help release tensions. Once you have mastered them, do them in a continuous flow like a dance. Work on coordinating breathing as indicated. Always breathe through the nose and exhale slowly.

1. Stand erect, arms alongside your body, feet slightly parted. Bring your hands together in the prayer position close to the upper chest, in salute to the god within and the energy that sustains you.

2. *Take a deep breath*, raise your arms overhead, upper arms touching ears, hands together high above head. Slowly bend backwards with beautiful control. Read the ceiling overhead. With practice, one day you will be able to read the wall behind you.

3. *Exhale*, bending forward. Grasp your ankles. Keep knees straight. Bring your face as close to your knees as possible. (At first you may not be able to grasp the ankles. Bend forward gently as far as you can without strain. In time the hamstrings will stretch and allow a full bend.)

4. Rise up, hands alongside body. Place your right foot forward and extend your left leg back, left knee on the ground, hands on either side of the right foot. *Inhale,* raise your head, stretching neck and turning face to look at the ceiling. Arch your back gently.

5. Without moving your hands, *retain breath* and move right leg back keeping your body straight.

6. *Exhale* slowly as you place knees, chest and forehead on the ground, spreading hands and lowering upper arms. Keep buttocks slightly raised.

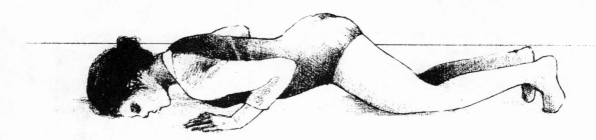

7. *Inhale*, lower knees and slowly raise your face up to the ceiling. Keep your arms slightly bent and pubic arch firmly on the ground.

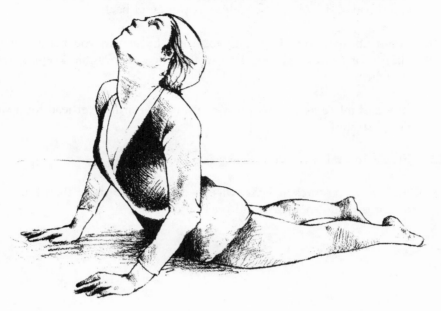

8. *Exhale* keeping your hands firmly placed, with toes on the ground, raise your buttocks up toward the wall behind you and press your heels toward the ground.

9. *Inhale* as you bring your left foot forward and extend your right leg back with right knee on the ground. Place hands beside your left foot, raise your head and look at the ceiling as you bend back.

10. Stand up and bring both legs together. *Exhale*, as you bend down to clasp your ankles, face as close to the knees as possible keeping knees straight.

11. Rise and *inhale* as you bend back raising your arms overhead for a wonderful stretch.

12. *Exhale* and relax to original prayer position.

Do these twelve postures at least twice, working up to three then four repetitions. Afterwards lie down, relax, and breathe deeply.

For the Legs

Do the following movements in the order indicated. At first do only as much as feels comfortable, but work until you are able to do them all perfectly with control and without strain. This series aids in firming the legs, thighs, and abdomen, and in releasing tension and keeping the body supple.

1. Lie flat on your back, stretch arms comfortably overhead, resting them on the floor. Throughout, remember to point your toes when extending the leg. To the count of four, bring the right leg up slowly as far as it will go without bending either knee. When it is perpendicular to the body begin to lower it, counting slowly: 1,2,3,4. Now the left leg up slowly to the count of four, and down: 1,2,3,4. Bring both legs up: 1,2,3,4, and down again to the ground to the count of 4.

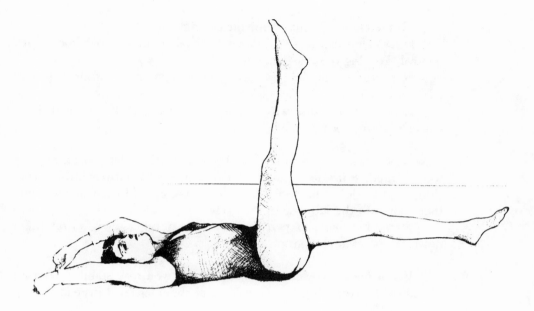

2. On your back, arms still stretched comfortably overhead, bring the right leg up perpendicular to the count of: 1,2,3 4. Swing the leg down to the right side of your body, keeping knee straight and toes pointed: 1,2,3,4.

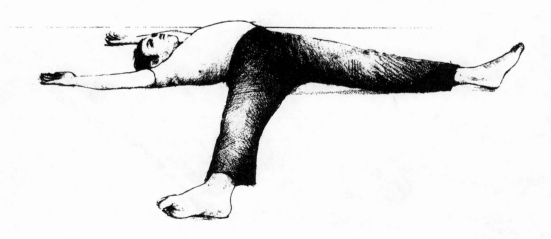

To the count of four again, lift the right leg slowly.

Now swing it across and down to the left side of your body, with control, keeping the knee straight: 1,2,3,4.

Bring the leg up and back down to the ground in front of you to the count of four.

Repeat the exercise with the left leg, again to the count of four. Knees straight, toes pointed.

3.   Now repeat with both legs without a count. Keep legs together with toes pointed. Raise legs perpendicular and slowly, with control, swing to the right side of the body. Raise legs back up and then slowly swing them down to the left side of the body.

Straighten legs up perpendicular, then *very* slowly bring them down to the ground in front of you.

If you find this exercise difficult at first you may stabilize yourself by extending your arms on the ground at shoulder level instead.

Remain flat on the floor for a minute and take several deep breaths.

4.   Still on your back, bring arms comfortably overhead again. Lift both legs up perpendicular, pause, then stretch legs wide apart, and bring them together.

Again stretch your legs apart, this time bending your knees. Bring knees together and straighten your legs up again.

Keeping upper body and head on the ground reach up and try to take hold of your ankles. Keep your knees straight!

At first you might not reach the ankles. Grasp the calves instead, but keep trying until you can eventually grasp the ankles. This creates a wonderful stretch for the spine.

Holding the ankles, spread the legs wide apart and then together; apart again; and together.

Continue holding ankles and bring your knees toward your chest. Lift your forehead up toward your knees and, with heels on buttocks, begin to rock in this position. Rock forward and back gently, two or three times.

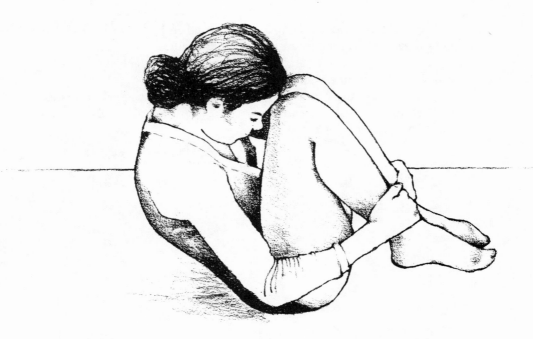

After rocking, return your head to the ground. Keep a hold on your ankles and straighten the legs again for a last, gentle pull on your spine.

Release your ankles and then, slowly, *to the count of four* lower your legs and move your arms back to the original overhead position. Relax a moment.

Bring arms to your sides and take several calm breaths.

Rocking

This is fun and most beneficial for a flexible spinal column. It is particularly good for blood circulation. I also believe it combats aging, as most back problems arise from a stiffened, inflexible spinal column. However, remember not to strain. Rocking should be done in a relaxed and masterful manner, and in time will become as important as brushing your teeth or combing your hair.

Sit on the floor and bring your knees to your chest. Clasp hands together under your knees and rock back.

As you do, straighten your legs so that your feet touch the ground behind your head.

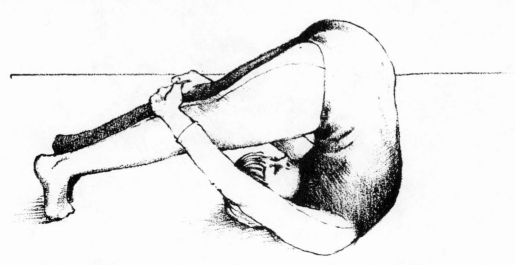

Rock back to the sitting position and repeat seven or eight times at the same gentle speed.

At first your legs may not be able to touch the ground behind you; this will depend on your physical condition. Do not be discouraged. As you rock bring your straightened legs as far back as possible. Work until you master this. The benefits are endless.

A Variation
Sit with your ankles crossed; take hold of your feet. Keeping your ankles crossed rock back and touch your toes on the ground behind your head. This time, do not straighten the legs.

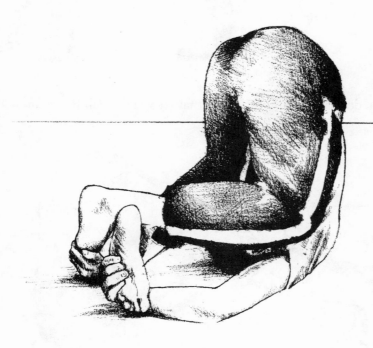

Keeping the position, rock back up and forward and touch your forehead to the ground in front. Do this five times or more.

Now lie down and relax, legs and arms spread, eyes closed. Breathe through your nose, slowly drawing each breath from your diaphragm.

Headstand

A word of caution. In revising this book, I have come to realize, along with others, that the benefits of the headstand are debatable. Though a superlative exercise, it is a difficult position, one that should be performed only by those who devote a great deal of time to yoga. For those with neck problems, the shoulderstand is a wise alternative.

You should never attempt the headstand unassisted. In my mid-twenties, when working with Ida, my first yoga teacher, it was a great challenge and took weeks of practice to master. If you decide to incorporate the headstand into your daily practice, believe you can do it but take your time and carefully practice parts one and two before starting part three. Always have someone assist you. Do not strain or force yourself no matter how strong or limber you may be.

Aside from its excellent physical benefits, the headstand can also be used as a posture for concentration. This exercise needs to be done step by step, with perfect control and balance. The patience is as valuable as the act.

1. Kneel and sit back on your heels, knees and feet together, stomach and buttocks firm. Clasp your hands gently and place them on the ground in front of you making a triangle with your hands and elbows.

Place the top of the head into the cup of your hands. Straighten your legs and walk toward your torso until your buttocks are directly over your head. Pause and feel this position.

2. Carefully let your feet leave the ground, moving the weight of your body onto your head and hands. As you lift up, bend your knees to your chest. Hold this position until you are balanced and in control.

3. Slowly extend your legs up, reaching for the sky.

In extending your legs, you can use a wall for a prop until you feel confident enough to do this without aid. Always take care to keep the body aligned and your weight evenly balanced without undue stress on the head, neck, shoulders, or arms. Do not strain. Practice until you can remain comfortably in this position for three to five minutes. Remember, it is *how* you do this exercise that counts.

For further challenge do the following while in the headstand: Stretch your legs wide apart, then bring them together.

Continue, bringing the right leg forward, left leg back. Then bring them together.

Then alternate, left leg forward, right leg back, and together.

Now bend your knees and cross your ankles. Slowly bring your knees down to your chest. Hold this position for five seconds.

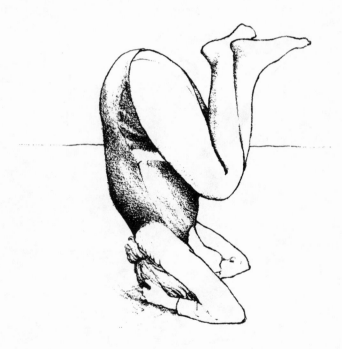

Calmly, straighten up, legs together with toes pointed toward the ceiling.

When coming down from the headstand it is extremely important to maintain control. First bend your knees toward your chest and slowly come down and place your feet on the ground, moving the weight of your body onto the feet.

Bend to your knees and lower your buttocks to your heels. Keep your head on the ground for thirty seconds or so until the blood in your body equalizes, then stretch out on your back and relax. Close your eyes and congratulate yourself.

Shoulderstand

This exercise helps strengthen the back and stimulates blood flow to the head and upper body. It is especially useful for those who may be uncomfortable with the headstand. If you desire you may use a folded blanket or towel, or even a slim pillow beneath your head to protect your neck. Execute extra care with the shoulderstand. Slow and gentle is the rule.

1. Lie on your back, arms at your sides, palms down, legs together. With toes pointed, raise your legs while lifting both the buttocks and hips up. Keep the lower body erect and stable by using your arms and hands to prop your back. At this point, your chin should be resting on your chest. In this position, your legs and trunk are perpendicular, stomach and hips aligned.

If you find it difficult to maintain this position, bring your legs down slightly and prop your hips on your hands.

The shoulderstand is an excellent way to relieve aching legs and feet, and flush the face with extra blood.

Hold the stand as long as possible and breathe deeply. Keeping the left leg straight up, bring the right leg down to the ground behind your head. Keep both knees straight. Pause, then bring the left leg down. Slowly swing both legs up to the perpendicular position.

2. While still in the shoulderstand bring both legs down to the ground behind your head. Point your toes and keep knees straight.

Slowly bring your legs up to shoulderstand. Repeat this lowering and raising of your legs behind the head.

3.   While still in the shoulderstand with toes pointed directly toward the ceiling, spread legs wide apart and bring both down behind your head.

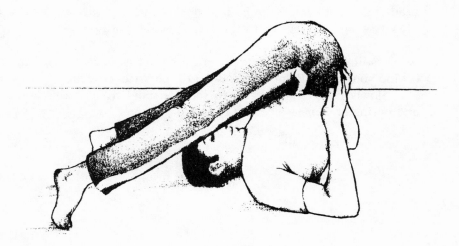

Return the right leg up first, then the left leg, keeping knees straight. Now bring legs together.

4.   Using your hands and arms to help the transfer of your weight, lower your body inch by inch, keeping your head on the ground as you do this.

Turn palms up; close your eyes and relax, breathing slowly.

Half Fish

This exercise stretches the neck, stimulates the thyroid, and brings extra blood to the face. It's especially good for the skin.

Lie on your back, palms down and under your buttocks. Gently arch your back until the top of your head touches the ground.

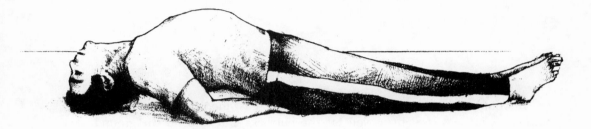

Now lift your right leg up, then the left leg, toes pointed toward the ceiling.

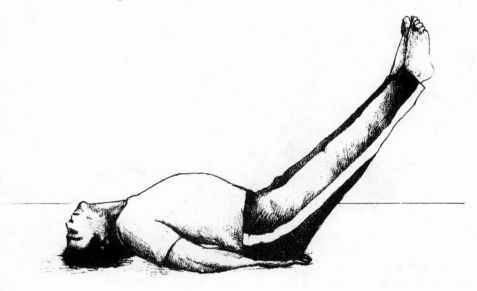

Lower both legs halfway to the ground; *the slower you do this the better.* Then lower them all the way down to the ground.

After a pause, bend back even further until the very top of your head touches the ground. This action stimulates the thyroid. Slowly relax your back; release your hands and breathe easy.

Plow

It would be best to attempt this in stages. It is important to take your time and keep your legs straight as you lift the buttocks and hips off the ground. Try not to bend your knees.

1. Lie on your back, legs together, arms alongside your body, palms down. Keeping your legs straight, lift them up over your head until your toes touch the ground behind you.

Straighten your knees for maximum benefit as you bring your legs behind your head. Do this with balance and control. Try to touch your toes to the ground. Try to hold this plow position for a count of ten.

2. Slowly raise both legs straight up in the air, then lower them letting your toes touch the ground behind your head. Repeat.

Reach back and take hold of your ankles and pull your legs wide apart, then together, and apart again.

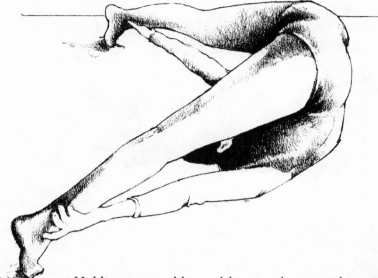

Holding your ankles and keeping legs straight, rock up into a sitting position and back down.

Bring legs together with toes on the ground behind your head. Remain in the plow position.

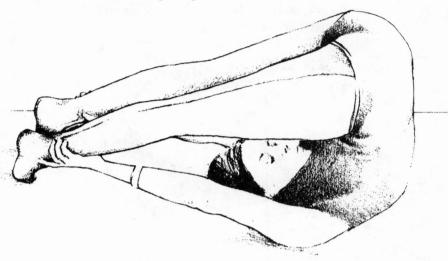

3. From the plow, bend your knees and wrap your arms over the backs of your knees so the palms of your hands are on your ears.

Take a deep breath in and exhale. Repeat. Remain in this position for at least ten seconds.

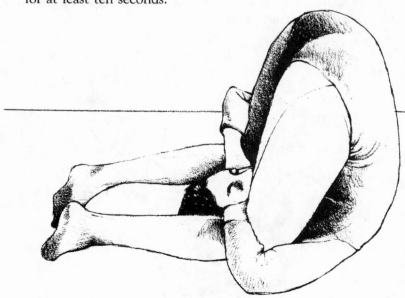

4. Return to the plow position and bring your arms back over your head, parallel to your legs. Keeping your arms on the ground, begin to lower your body slowly, vertebra by vertebra. Inch your way down. Keep tightening the small of your back and your stomach muscles. Point your toes, keeping legs very straight all of the way.

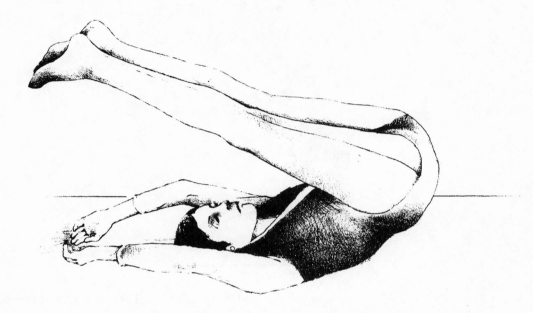

  Try not to lose control as your buttocks get close to the ground. This part of the exercise is especially good for strengthening the back.
  Relax, with your arms still over your head, and take a few deep breaths.

Plow Combination

1. Lie on your back, with your arms on the ground over your head. Begin to sit up, reaching for the sky.

Tuck in your stomach, bend further, and try to take hold of your ankles. Your elbows should be on the ground. Gently work this position until your forehead touches your knees.

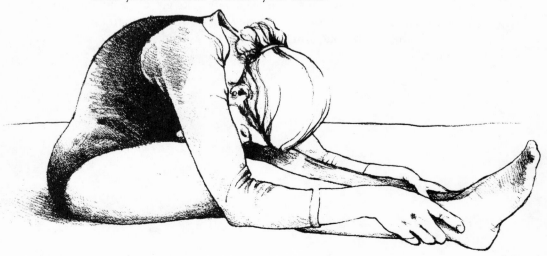

Move your stomach in and out several times as you inhale and exhale.

Release your ankles and slowly sit up, arms reaching for the sky. Counting, take thirty seconds to lie back down. Be aware of the muscles in your back. Try not to let your heels leave the ground.

This is a fine exercise for balance and is wonderful for the stomach. Relax for a few seconds and breathe deeply.

2. Lying on your back with your arms on the ground over your head, resume the plow position in one smooth swing. Keep the knees straight!

Now spread your legs wide apart behind your head and, pointing your toes to the wall behind, come down slowly, vertebra by vertebra. Keep your hands on the ground behind your head and maintain control.

Relax for several deep breaths.

3. Now sit up, with legs spread in front of you. Reach for the sky with your hands then gently bend forward placing your right hand on the right ankle, and your left hand on the left ankle. Bend as far as you can without strain. Try to place your forehead on the ground.

4. Sit up and remain sitting with your legs spread. Clasp both hands on your right ankle and gently bend forward. Try placing your forehead on your right knee.

Sit up. Repeat for the left leg, with your hands on your left ankle, forehead on your left knee, keeping knees straight as possible.

Sit up again. Now move the right hand to the right toes and the left hand to the left toes; be courageous and bend down even further, ever so gently, as you try to place your forehead on the ground between your legs.

Once more, sit up, bringing both legs together in front of you. Place your hands on the ground alongside your hips, with your palms down.

Raise your body straight up and drop your head back. Push your stomach up toward the ceiling.

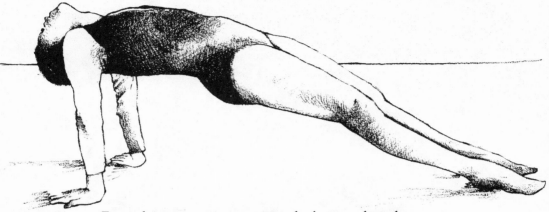

From this position raise your right leg up, then down. Now raise the left leg up, and down.

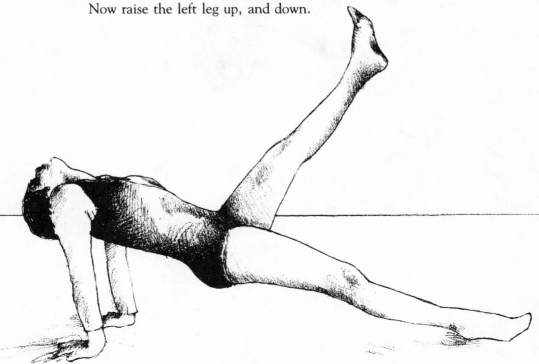

Raise your right arm up, then down.
Raise your left arm up, then down.

Slowly lie down and relax.
Take sixty seconds of complete relaxation and feel what you have
done for yourself.

The Rise

Lie on your stomach, forehead on the ground, hands alongside your shoulders. Do this exercise to the count of nine.

Inhale slowly, raise your head to the count of 1,2,3—now shoulders up to 4,5,6—and begin to straighten your elbows, lifting your face up parallel to the ceiling with 7,8,9. Keep your pubic arch firmly on the ground as you bend the small of your back.

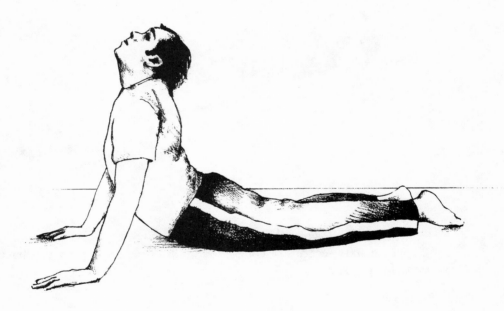

Exhale coming down slowly—1,2,3,4,5,6,7 and head down to the count of 8,9. Do not bring your face down before the count of 7.

Repeat the exercise.

Cradle your head in your arms and relax.

For the Stomach

1. Kneel with your knees apart, your back straight and the tops of your feet on the ground.

    Squeeze your shoulder blades together as you drop your head back.

    Push your stomach forward and place hands on your heels. The key to this exercise is squeezing the shoulder blades together. Keep buttocks tucked in as you hold this position for a count of four, then return to starting position.

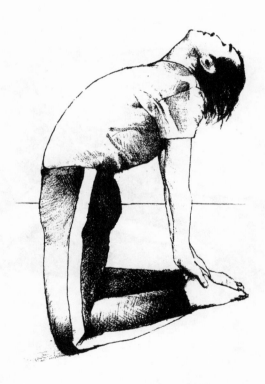

2. Kneel with your knees apart.

Sit back, grasp your heels and slowly bend forward placing the top of your head on the ground in front of you.

3. Rise to your knees and again squeeze the shoulder blades together. Drop your head back as you grasp your ankles pushing your stomach forward. This makes for an even greater stretch.

4. Rise to your knees and sit back down on your heels. Grasp your heels as you lower your chin to the ground. Extend the spine.

5. Rise to your knees and place your hands on your hips. Slowly bend backwards until your head touches the ground behind you. Use your elbows for support.

Work your way back down to the ground and cross your arms on your chest.

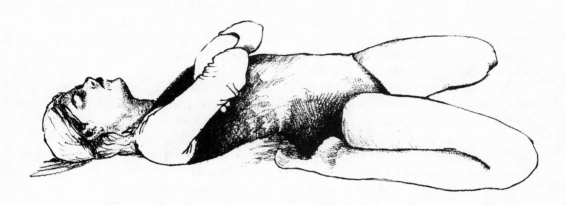

In this posture, inhale and exhale slowly. Now in complete control of your body, rise to a sitting position. This is difficult at first, but you will master it if you keep trying.

Release arms and legs and lie down to rest.

Breathing

Few of us realize that breathing needs exercise. Most breathing we do is what is termed "clavicular," or shallow breathing, which tends to deny the body an optimum oxygen supply. Breathing exercises correct this fault. They can be done anywhere, but should be done slowly, especially after completing an exercise sequence. The benefits are cumulative. By conscious attention to correct posture you can reduce stress and energize your entire system. To improve the breath is to improve life. Breathing exercises are a device for improving physical, mental, and spiritual capacities. To gain the levels of awareness you seek, a regular practice of correct breathing is invaluable.

Four breathing exercises follow. When practicing them, sit comfortably on a chair or sofa, or on the floor cross-legged. However you choose to sit, keep knees lower than hips to allow free diaphragm movement. Your torso and head need to be erect to allow maximum lung capacity. Relax your shoulders and neck. As you breathe in and out through the nose, feel the air passing across the air passages behind your nostrils. Be aware of this subtle sensation. Breathing in, expand your abdomen, diaphragm, and chest in that order. Reverse when exhaling. Imagine breath like a circle of air coming in and going out. Never force breath or make yourself rigid with air. Try to keep the shoulders and arms relaxed and still. Breathe naturally and be aware of the center of your body, just below the navel. Feel the force of life entering your body, filling every cell with renewed energy. Be conscious of directing this dynamic energy.

1.   Sneezing and Clearing the Lungs

This exercise may seem similar to hyperventilating except you are not concerned with filling your lungs with oxygen but rather with making an effort to clear the air from your lungs.

Sit with back and head aligned. (It might be advisable to keep tissues at hand.) Sneeze only through the nose. Each time you expel air pull in your stomach. Do forty fast expulsions. Remember, nothing should move except the stomach. Keep your shoulders still.

Inhale and count as you sneeze, 1-2-3-4-5-6-7-8-9-10 all the way to 40! Then pause, inhale deeply, and slowly exhale.

Again, as above, do fifteen sneezing expulsions, but this time much slower and harder. Sneeze so that you can hear yourself.

Inhale and count as you sneeze, 1-2-3-4-5 through 15.

Inhale deeply, exhale, and relax for twenty seconds as your breath becomes normal.

2. Changing Air

In this exercise you exhale more than you inhale in order to clear dead air from the lungs.

Inhale 1-2-3-4-5.

Exhale 1-2-3-4-5-6-7-8-9-10.

Repeat.

This time inhale to the count of *ten* and exhale to the count of *twelve*.

Inhale 1-2-3-4-5-6-7-8-9-10.

Exhale 1-2-3-4-5-6-7-8-9-10-11-12.

Relax and breathe normally.

3. Breath Retention

Sit erect but comfortable and relaxed. Inhale slightly more deeply than normal, but don't make yourself rigid with air. Practice will help. The important thing is not to force breath retention so that you expel the air all at once.

Inhale 1-2-3-4-5 and hold for forty-five seconds.

Think of the good you do for yourself by bringing extra oxygen to the blood, the nerves and skin. Feel yourself gaining strength.

Exhale 1-2-3-4-5-6-7-8-9-10.

Relax and breathe normally.

Try again, this time holding the breath for sixty seconds.

Inhale 1-2-3-4-5.

For one minute, as you hold your breath, calmly visualize the pleasant day or evening to come during the weekend ahead, the change that will take place. You may meet someone important to you, perhaps do a small kindness for someone in need. Feel strong and create a victory in this moment of quiet.

Exhale slowly 1-2-3-4-5-6-7-8-9-10.

Relax.

4. Alternate Nostril Breathing

I feel this is the best breathing exercise for relaxation. It can be used as an antidote to anger, agitation, nervousness, or insomnia. The more you do, the more you benefit. *It is important to follow the cumulative count in this exercise.*

Make a fist of your right hand and extend the thumb and index finger. Place the thumb over the right nostril and inhale through the left nostril. Inhale 1-2-3-4-5. Close both nostrils to retain breath 1-2-3-4-5.

Release the thumb and exhale through the right nostril 1-2-3-4-5.

Keep the left nostril closed with your index finger and inhale through the right nostril 1-2-3-4-5-6.

Close both nostrils and retain the breath 1-2-3-4-5-6.

Release the left nostril and exhale 1-2-3-4-5-6.

Inhale through left nostril 1-2-3-to-7.

Close nostrils and retain breath 1-2-3-to-7.

Release the right nostril and exhale 1-2-3-to-7.

Inhale through right nostril 1-2-3-to-8.

Close nostrils and retain breath 1-2-3-to-8.

Release the left nostril and exhale 1-2-3-to-8.

Inhale through left nostril 1-2-3-to-9.

Close nostrils and retain breath 1-2-3-to-9.

Release the right nostril and exhale 1-2-3-to-9.

Inhale through right nostril 1-2-3-to-10.

Close nostrils and retain breath 1-2-3-4.

Release the left nostril and exhale 1-2-3-to-10.

Inhale through left nostril 1-2-3-to-10.

Close nostrils and retain breath 1-2-3-4.

Release the right nostril and exhale 1-2-3-to-10.

Inhale through right nostril 1-2-3.

Close nostrils and retain breath 1-2-3-4-5.

Release the left nostril and exhale 1-2-3-to-8.

Inhale through left nostril 1-2-3.

Close nostrils and retain breath 1-2-3-4-5.

Release your thumb and exhale through right nostril 1-2-3-to-8.

This regimen is a wondrous, natural system that soothes and relaxes. You will feel the results immediately.

For the Eyes

The following exercises are simple, yet they can make us aware of the fact that we can improve our vision. Concern for vision enhancement has become more sophisticated as we begin to understand that good vision does not just happen. According to Marc Grossman, a psychobehavioral optometrist, "Good vision involves our entire self"; our awareness of space, sound, and touch, as well as how we speak, listen and think determine what we see in front of us.

Sit comfortably erect. Keep the head and shoulders still; move only the eyes.

1. Place your index finger at arm's length. Keep your eyes focused on your finger, bringing the finger toward you until it touches your nose. Let your gaze follow your finger as you extend it to arm's length again. Repeat this in-and-out focus at least ten times.

2. Stare ahead. Lift your gaze to a spot on the ceiling directly above you, then look down to the ground in front of you. Look up at the ceiling again, then down. Repeat the up-down-motion ten times.
    Close your eyes for thirty seconds and breathe deeply.

3. Open your eyes. Snap your gaze to the far right and back to the far left. Repeat this sweep at least ten times.
    Close your eyes for thirty seconds and breathe deeply.

4. Open your eyes and stare ahead. Now, as if following the circumference of a large gold circle, let your eyes begin from the bottom, circling your gaze toward the right, up, around to the left and down. *Do not move your head.* Begin again at the bottom and circle to the left, rolling your eyes slowly up, then right, and around. Repeat this exercise ten times.
    Look forward and gently place the palms of your hands over your closed eyes. Breathe deeply.
    Later, as you get more proficient in these eye exercises, you may wish to extend the number of repetitions.

These exercises strengthen the eye muscles and may even halt the progressive deterioration of eyesight or the need for stronger glasses. Activating the rods and cones in the eye through exercise can result in wider, heightened vision.

For the Neck

Sit comfortably with back straight, keeping shoulders relaxed and motionless. Nothing should move except your head.

1. Gently turn your face all the way to the right, then forward, then to the left, then forward. Repeat twice. Now tilt the head to the right shoulder, then up. Tilt to the left, then up. Repeat this twice. After a pause, without moving your shoulders, extend the face and neck forward. (The movement is similar to the movement of a turtle's head.) Move your head backward and forward two or three times.

2. With your eyes closed, drop your chin to your chest and do some neck rolls. First roll your head gently to the right shoulder and back, then to the left shoulder, forward and down.

    Now gently roll your head to the left shoulder, back, to the right shoulder, forward and down.

    Repeat the neck rolls slowly two or three times.

3. While sitting on the ground, with your head erect and eyes open, lean forward and place your elbows on the ground with your hands cupping your face as you stare at the wall ahead. Feel the pull on your spinal column. Hold this position for thirty seconds.

    Sit up and repeat.

Now sit comfortably again and relax.

Going Within

Going Within is an ancient idea, the revival of which has been questionably modernized. The actualization of *Going Within* has countless variations. The exercise here is a variation of the yogic "corpse asana." I recommend it as a last step to any exercise sequence. It can be done anyplace, anytime and, exclusive of exercise, it is marvelous before dinner or bed. When relaxation is needed during a crisis it provides unbelievable benefits. Properly practiced, it might well be as complete a means of relaxation as any devised, for it transcends the physical by relieving tension, calming muscles, and soothing the nervous system. It is a way of rearranging the senses and producing a removal which generates renewed energy. It melts the body away so that the mind is free to experience relief.

Some people who are troubled by a physical disability use this exercise for meditation. That takes extensive practice. Nonetheless, for the faithful practitioner *Going Within* brings a unification of physical and emotional selves which once begun will not be easily abandoned.

Ideally, this exercise should be done for fifteen or twenty minutes. A flat, comfortable surface is necessary. The body must lie on a straight plane. A soft carpet is probably best. I list this exercise last because it might be appropriate to shower and then return to finish the sequence by *Going Within*.

In any case, take several deep breaths before lying down. Rotate your arms and twist the trunk of your body as you stand. When you lie down on your back keep up the slightly exaggerated breathing as you spread your arms and legs. Keep the palms of your hands up as you settle your head and shoulders so that your neck is in line with your spine. Relax your jaw muscles but keep your lips closed and, as always, breathe from the stomach and only through your nose.

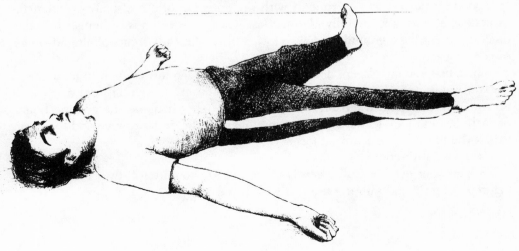

Close your eyes. Roll your body gently from side to side. Adjust the angle of your arms and legs, spreading them at the same angle from your torso. After some practice the best angle will become apparent.

Check that no clothing binds you; loosen a tight belt or collar. Make sure you cover yourself so that you are comfortably warm, and stay clear of drafts.

As you begin to relax, suffer any itch or irritation. Once you begin do not move or open your eyes. Quiet the body. Let go. Let the stomach do the breathing. Slow the breath. After practice you will become familiar enough with the rhythm of your heart to be able to slow that as well.

Allow the waves of tension to rise and evaporate. Continually release your hands and neck and face. This process can be repeated over and over again. One of the mysteries of *Going Within* is to discover the complex layers of tension within the body. After the basic technique is mastered it is sometimes surprising to feel so perfectly still and then be delicately shaken by deeper unexpected relaxation.

Last, and most difficult, let go of the brain. Allow the emergencies, the responsibilities, errands, and important calls to dissolve . . . along with things to buy, laundry to be done, letters to be written . . . and the never-ending, multi-dimensional parade of petty urgencies that plague you.

Follow the slow rise and fall of your stomach as it breathes. After a few minutes you can reduce that breathing and begin simple visualizations: a diamond soaring into the distance or turning circles that revolve around each breath. Let your brain clear and begin to rest.

Once centered, never move.

Slip like a sleeping child into the secure arms of the strong, the loved, the safe shelter into which no thought can intrude.

Once mastered, *Going Within* can be used for more sophisticated unification. It is good for beginning experiments with the potential of out-of-body experience, or beneficial during a carefully planned fast when the demands of hunger become onerous. It can be a grounding device for realizing the early limits of altered states of consciousness.

If at first you fall asleep, do. You will probably sleep just enough to fill a need. As you wake up and come back, do so slowly. You are returning from a magical reverie. Let the mind dwell on a healing white light. Imagine the coming hours of each day and look forward to reflecting love and the desire to give and to learn; this is the finest act you can perform.

Remain still; come back slowly.

Open your eyes carefully, gently stretch, and carefully roll over on your side before sitting up and saluting the god within you.

III.

Only by regular exercise can anyone begin to achieve a greater sense of the reality of the body. We need to be serious about exercise. The true reason we exercise is that we seek to bring a vast change to daily existence and the inevitable process of aging. Recent research in longevity proves that exercise is a vital element of well-being in later years. We need to see that those routines we developed at the age of thirty or forty can still be maintained at sixty or seventy. We harbor dangerous illusions with regard to our bodies. Most overweight people live under the illusion that they are "really not too heavy." A greater number of people feel that their health is "generally good." Regular exercise gradually breaks through these veils of our physical reality and reveals the many different, subtle versions of the self that are seldom recognized or understood. These variations are often overlooked because of the temptations of success, or the need for sex and/or love. They are ignored because of the demands of work, family, community, or energy devoted to the needs of the earth. In such collective confusion the individual psyche is split off, even alienated from its psychosomatic ground. Inherent integrity is violated. Disorder and disease threaten personal well-being. Carefully planned and faithfully executed exercise not only insures a fresh perspective on such confusion but provides other benefits as well.

An important benefit for me was discovering how exercise combined with regulated consumption and meditative practice became a powerful antidote to loneliness. This promoted the kind of change that occurs with the sensible unification of awareness. Dealing with loneliness, existentially acting against self-alienation, produced in me a new poise. Unifying awareness was a way to dissolve a core of loneliness that had affected me more than I realized. The new-found confidence was exhilarating. This is probably the reason why so many millions of Americans have begun to run, walk, or experiment with yoga and aerobics. Getting in touch with one's physical body is the surest way to end up feeling good about who you are. The much-revered "runner's high" and all its gradations can be self-generated elixirs of life. Combining the impetus this provides with an overall goal of unifying awareness is what Jack Schwarz calls "the path of action." Properly planned, it is a sure way toward true change.

But go easy. Remember not to strain or force yourself. Above all, be personally comfortable and pamper yourself with the time you have created to initiate the body, the mind, and the place into revolutionary holistic longevity.

And do not stop.

This is only a beginning.

3.

The Lifetime Diet

E*ach being has only one body, and he may choose to nourish that body with the foods that grow in the earth, or he may choose to have someone else harvest the earthy food, process it, add chemicals to it, preserve it, put it into a plastic bag, put that plastic bag into a box, call it new, tell us that it will taste good, and most incredibly, tell us that it is food that will sustain our bodies when we eat it.*

Ellen Buchman Ewald
Recipes for a Small Planet

I.

Regular exercise and improved breathing techniques will improve the health of your body and help to relieve the accumulated tensions of stress. But without paying keen attention to every area of consumption we are far from the goal of awareness. We are not only what we eat and drink as food, but also what we breathe. What we see and hear and otherwise take into and process within ourselves also affects us. The chapter on lifestyle considers how to identify and rid your environment of polluting or energy-sapping items of the non-food variety; in this chapter we consider food and basic eating habits.

The disadvantage of living in an industrialized society is that we are far removed from the earth and completely dependent on transportation and technology for food. Despite a phenomenal increase in dietary awareness, the sad truth is that most people do not know how to eat properly; that is, to obtain the nutrients they

73

require in the correct amounts and proportions. It is still confusing and difficult to understand the true importance of proper diet. Even concerned individuals follow tastes which usually have been grossly manipulated by food technology and advertising, and habitually eat too much food of questionable nutritional quality. The overfed, undernourished body becomes a sluggish body, and is a constant drain on vital energy. Sooner or later that body will fall into *dis-ease*, showing early signs of trouble and disintegration.

To free the body and mind to develop awareness and expand consciousness we must acquire an acute sense of what we consume. We need to learn what a sound diet is, and to awaken our individual "body wisdom" that intuits the body's needs. Acting on this information coupled with this kind of sensitivity, we will bring about lasting changes of increased well-being. We will become lighter, more energized, more responsive to life, and more able to explore other realms of awareness. The changes will be relative at first, depending on the individual, but steady effort guarantees success.

To begin, we need to eliminate the promise of dieting, of eating a certain way for a certain period of time before returning to habits of consumption that caused trouble in the first place. We need only note the insane number of plain and fancy diets, dietary aides, schemes, and gimmicks in order to realize the futility of dieting in the traditional way. Fads abound, each one seemingly contradicting the next. This or that product becomes fashionable, is promoted by a well-known authority, or chewed on television by a famous personality or an Olympic athlete. We sometimes devour the absurdity by eating only three grapefruits a day, or six hard-boiled eggs and half a head of lettuce, or nothing but lean red meat and bottled water. Usually all we are trying to do is lose weight in order to improve our appearance and correct a physical condition we know to be unhealthy. Yet we practice illusions. For a certain period of time—the weekend crash diet, the 21-day/10 pounds-away plan—we eat only certain things in strictly limited amounts, counting calories and bravely trying to ignore hunger pangs. We try an all-fruit diet for a week or an all-protein diet, but when that period is over we slide back into habits that made us overweight in the first place. Yoyo-ing the body back and forth to the tune of the dietary experts is not only asinine but dangerous to health. Further, it insults the body's ability to regulate itself and demeans control of the self.

There should be only one diet. A final, lifetime diet. The key to this way of eating is to become knowledgeable about the *quality* of food you eat, and learning to *prepare* your own food.

A lifetime diet is a plan of food consumption and a pattern of eating habits to be followed for the rest of one's life. It is not a diet that can only be adopted when a certain amount of weight is lost or a certain level of health is obtained. It is a control of consumption that avoids the hypocrisy of traditional dieting and brings eating into a sensible range. As one gradually develops and settles into a lifetime diet, the body becomes properly nourished and gradually finds its best weight. This will usually be far less than one thought.

Make the transition into a final lifetime diet subtly, step by step. It can be shocking if gone into rashly. Change should never be treated lightly. Remember the sort of change you seek is long range. To break old habits and formulate a new discipline you will need to proceed patiently, slowly, and surely.

Becoming aware of your own food preferences and eating habits is a prerequisite for changing them. One good way to do this is to use a small notebook that fits easily into a purse or hip pocket in which to keep a record of everything you eat and drink each day. Do this for a few days every week for eight or ten weeks. Begin this record once you have started the exercise practices outlined in the preceding chapter. Don't be concerned with exact quantities—approximations will suffice—or be bothered by looking up calorie counts. But try to record whether the food was commercially preserved—frozen or processed—or freshly prepared from natural products. With bread and crackers, note whether the flour was refined or whole grain. With dairy products, note whether the food was full-fat, low-fat, or non-fat. Remember to record snacks, whether you've had a candy bar, a piece of fruit, potato chips with a drink before dinner, or a glass of milk at bedtime. Of course, when you eat a restaurant meal it is usually impossible to find out the source of the food on your plate, but you might ask in a friendly manner and you will probably be surprised by what you learn.

At the end of this recording period, when you have established the discipline of exercise and keeping the food diary to use as the basis for change, you will be ready to institute a lifetime diet. You will learn the value of limiting what you eat and experience the satisfaction to be gained from it. The transition might require many months before it is complete; challenge but do not deprive yourself. Advance steadily toward your goal. In the eyes of family members or friends your efforts might seem odd or corny, but ignore the negative reactions of others. After all, your health and well-being is your responsibility. Follow the guidelines you have established and revise them when necessary. A lifetime diet is not a fad; it need not restrict or confine you to rigid consumption. Rather, it will impart discrimination to your eating habits. As the exercises put you in touch with the physical reality of your body, new patterns of consumption will begin to put you in touch with the quality of your energy. Your intuition concerning your body's needs will be awakened and the process of refining self-awareness will gain momentum.

This process has actually begun once we acknowledge that what and how much we eat makes the difference between burdening or releasing the self, between staying in the darkness of procrastination or rising naturally into the light of awareness. "You are what you eat" extends to what you see and hear. It extends to what you do, and to what you desire. Greater awareness can start with a simple appreciation of the value of fresh food as opposed to junk or convenience foods. Expanding such awareness can make the difference between the later years of life being lost in senility or spent in vibrant health with the capacity for using wisdom and age, the capacity to *experience* rather than suffer death.

Do not hesitate. Heed your best instincts and resolve now to fulfill your desire for sane consumption. At thirty or forty years of age it is already difficult to change long-standing habits; by sixty or sixty-five, breaking old habits becomes a real challenge.

> **B**etween the fresh, natural, whole food and its refined, fractioned commercial product there is an abyss of lost nourishment, even when the refined food has been enriched. In whole foods there is a balance between calories and other nutrients, a certain density of nourishment that is lacking in many refined foods. The basic requirements of human nutrition are water, carbohydrate, protein, a broad range of vitamins and minerals, and a little fat or oil. Whole foods contribute to many of these needs at once; refined foods often contribute to only one or two.
>
> Laurel Robertson, Carol Flinders
> and Bronwen Godfrey
> *Laurel's Kitchen*

My own final diet began unobtrusively many years ago. It rose out of hunger for fresh foods. Like most people who lived alone, I had succumbed to the temptations of "easy eating." Convenience foods were so varied and handy that I lost incentive to prepare my own meals. It was so much easier to reach into the freezer compartment of the local supermarket and pick out a meal from a wide choice of frozen prepared dinners. When I wanted to treat myself to a nutritious meal, I would thaw out a frozen steak, throw it in the broiler, and make an effort at a salad. The salad usually consisted of a handful of lettuce, maybe a tomato, and bottled dressing.

I had already begun to travel a lot in those days and my eating habits reflected it. Every now and then I realized that I was making an uneasy compromise. Thinking myself too busy to shop daily for fresh foods as my mother had done, yet not wanting to be wasteful, I stuck with frozen meals and packaged and canned goods. Often my energy was low. I blamed it on jet lag, a hazard of my work. However, other doubts nagged at me. Sometimes after finishing a meal I suspected I had cheated myself.

Like most of my generation I grew up in a household that had never seen a TV-dinner or frozen steak. My mother went to the market daily (or sent me!) to purchase fresh vegetables, fish, or fruits. Beef at the time was an unusual treat. I was brought up on fish and, occasionally, a lamb dish. It was those meals I instinctively missed later, the wholesomeness of fresh food freshly prepared. I began to change my habits and put more effort into the preparation of meals even though it meant more trips to the market and more time in the kitchen.

For a long while this was an off-and-on thing that could hardly have been considered a new pattern of living. It was always dependent upon whether or not I had the time. Priorities were resistant to change. I felt new eating habits were important, but time was precious and hours were crammed with work and often lost in meaningless activity. With the benefit of hindsight I can say that I gave too much attention to relationships and involvements that sometimes proved superficial. To use a metaphor from Sufism, I was frittering away my life as a counterfeiter among other counterfeiters, hardly aware at all of genuine value. I spent too much time seeking companionship and rarely allowed myself to be alone. It was not until years later that I realized that I feared loneliness and for this reason sought the company of a certain friend or special situation. I now know that the friend I needed lives within, and the fulfilling situation is a feeling of wholeness in myself.

Back then, however, I had no idea how a change of eating habits could lead to other changes that would profoundly alter the way I lived and who I was. All I knew was that I hungered for fresh, unadulterated foods. What I learned over a period of many years I have distilled here as the guidelines for a lifetime diet.

A word of caution: some people have medical disorders that call for special diets. The lifetime diet might require adjustment for such people. As always, anyone with a medical condition should check with his or her doctor before undertaking any radical change in diet. However, for the average person without clinical problems, a sweeping change in food consumption in accordance with the guidelines offered here can be wholly beneficial to the creation or maintenance of a healthy body.

Let us start with what should *not* be consumed.

Those with a fondness for sweets find the idea of giving up sugar far from easy. It helps to realize that like tobacco and alcohol, *sugar is an addictive substance.* I discovered the facts about sugar in *Sugar Blues*, by William Dufty, a landmark book published in 1975. Although sugar is made from a natural source, 90% of the cane or beet is discarded during processing. What remains is a highly acidic, completely non-nutritive chemical molecule. Like so many other addictive substances, it rapidly enters the bloodstream and provides instant energy spurts that fizzle out as quickly as they come. Meanwhile, the sugar dose has lashed the adrenal and pancreatic glands into emergency action and whiplash effects are experienced all around the endocrine system. Dufty quotes endocrinologist J.W. Tintera on the unequivocally good results of a sugar-free diet: "It is quite possible to improve your personality for the better. The way to do it is to avoid cane and beet sugar in all its forms and guises." It is imperative to remember too that sugar is the major cause of tooth decay and a prime agent in fostering obesity. Recognition of this danger can be seen in the proliferation of "sugar-free" products.

A GOLDEN RULE

Consumption of sugar and refined-flour products should be dramatically reduced. Do not be misled by the promise of "raw sugar," or coarse brown sugar that sells at a premium price in many health-food stores. Sugar is sugar, and the object is to avoid it. White flour and white, or polished, rice are low-quality foods that have been stripped of most of their nutritional value and, apart from the quickly accessible fuel they provide, can only add weight to your body.

White flour and white rice are not in the same zero-nutrition category as sugar, but these foods have had the best part of their nourishment refined away. Generations of Europeans and Asians have used whole wheat and unpolished rice as staples of their diet. In their whole, unrefined state, these are high-quality foods; processed and devitalized, they mainly supply fuel and much ends up on your hips, thighs and belly as excess weight.

Ridding your diet of sugar, white rice and white-flour products such as breads, rolls, pastries, and pasta, may be difficult at first if you are not familiar with the alternatives.

Unfiltered honey can be used as a sweetener, but always in moderation. Though the mind often disagrees, the body has absolutely no need for sweets. The desire or craving for sweetness is an acquired taste that can be shed by patient attention to what we consume. Eat fresh fruit. It is a wonderfully delicious alternative. Or end a meal with an herbal tea sweetened with half a teaspoon of honey. Eat only brown or unpolished rice, which still has its nutrients. The French call it *riz complet*, and so it is: a complete food. Instead of foods made of white flour, favor those made from any whole-grain flour that has been stone ground, such as whole wheat or rye. In addition to their nourishment, whole grains also provide the fibrous roughage that facilitates your natural elimination processes. This is evident in the national attention given to bran and its introduction to cereal products readily available in major grocery and health-food stores.

While you deal with the problem of sugar, simultaneously cut back on the amount of fat you eat. This includes the butter or margarine on your bread as well as oil used in cooking and the fats found in meat, even the leanest cuts. Above all, cut back on your consumption of dairy products, especially milk and ice cream.

Nutritionists believe that the body requires certain fatty acids but they can only speculate on how much, or how little, fat in the diet is necessary to meet these requirements. In a comprehensive study begun in 1983 at Cornell University, nutritional biochemist T. Colin Campbell compared American and Chinese diets. One of the most tantalizing findings was that obesity is related more to what people eat than how much. The Chinese consume 20% more calories than Americans, but Americans are 25% fatter. In *Diet and Nutrition*, a work published in 1978 and still widely used, Rudolph Ballentine tells about a study made in India of a group whose total daily intake of fat per person was *less than a teaspoon* and who "presented no signs or symptoms which could be attributed to fat deficiency." Our average American diet contains up to twenty times this amount of fat. One can say that we Americans present many signs and symptoms of excessive fat consumption by pointing to the great number of overweight and obese people, the high incidence of hardening of the arteries (even among children and young adults), and the appalling cancer toll. Dr. Ballentine was one of the first to speculate that excess fat intake was one of the major causes of cancer. Today, fortunately, there is hardly any need to dwell on the great bugaboos of heart disease and cancer in this context.

You know that fat in your diet makes for fat on your body. Perhaps you also know that close to half the total fat in the average American diet comes from meat. For this reason alone, consider reducing your usual consumption of red meat and red-meat products. However you accomplish it, a lifetime diet calls for a major reduction in the amount of fat that you consume.

It is wise to eliminate as much as possible all processed and canned foods (except some canned fish). This includes all obvious convenience items as well as the expensive "gourmet" goods. Despite claims of being "natural," many processed foods are still loaded with sugar—also called dextrose, sucrose and cane syrup. Dozens of chemicals are added for easier packing and shipping and longer "shelf life," not for preserving nutritional value.

Be more alert. Read labels and learn what they mean. Throughout the 1980s consumer groups have extended your right to know exactly what you are getting when you buy prepared foods. Still, too many packaged and canned items are of dubious nutritional value even though they may taste good and have a modern appeal to those who have forgotten, or never known, the taste and appearance of natural foods. The manufacturers of processed food spend millions of dollars on advertising to convince the public that their products are good food. But slick color photos and the magic of audio-visual persuasion are dangerous guides.

Another questionable item still prominent in processed and canned foods is salt, along with sodium compounds. Salt is considered by many experts to be the single greatest cause of high blood pressure. According to heart specialist Lot Page, it is estimated that millions of Americans suffer from this disease, many without knowing it. Worse, it seems that hypertensives crave salt. Like sugar, salt is an addictive substance—the more one gets the more one wants. Dr. Page has long recommended less than a quarter teaspoon of salt a day, about one gram. A large pickle contains two grams of sodium; two ounces of processed cheese nearly one gram. Sodium is plentiful in dairy products, fish, and meat. The point is, you can easily get all the sodium your body needs without ever touching a salt shaker. The excessive amounts of sodium contained in processed and canned foods is another compelling reason to avoid them.

Instead of salt, use herbs to enhance the natural flavor of the foods you prepare. Use Vega-Salt, a seasoning which has been in health-food stores for years. A seasoning guide is included in this chapter. One of the best seasoning alternatives is to experiment more with garlic, a hearty and healthful food about which books have been written and songs have been sung! Small amounts go a long way. For seasoning soups and salads, add a sprinkling of finely chopped fresh parsley or chives just before serving. Fresh lemon juice adds zest to all fish and poultry dishes and does wonders for green vegetables too.

SEASONING GUIDE

Poultry: bay leaves, curry, ginger, marjoram, oregano, rosemary, sage, turmeric, saffron, savory, tarragon, thyme

Fish: allspice, bay leaves, celery seed, curry, marjoram, turmeric, mustard, oregano, sage, savory, tarragon, thyme

Shellfish: basil, bay leaves, chili powder, curry, marjoram

Tofu: miso, tamari (or shoyu), mirin, lemon, honey, celery seed, sesame seed, curry, basil, oregano, parsley

Cheese: caraway seed, cumin, ginger, mace, mustard, oregano, rosemary, sage

---

The alternative to eating foods processed by profit-making industries is, of course, to prepare your own food. Obviously this takes more time and energy, but if eating properly adds ten or twenty good years to life, how foolish it is to "save" an hour or so a day by eating convenience foods. Still, there is an even more important consideration. Shopping and cooking for yourself or your family will not seem such a tedious chore once you fully realize that those foodstuffs, lovingly and skillfully handled and prepared by you, literally become part of you and those with whom you share them. There is a joy in establishing communion with food. The pleasure in preparing wholesome meals arises from awareness of nurturing the health and purity of the self and others with whom you share your life. The care, the effort you make, can provide a vital ingredient that not only enhances the meal but brings an intangible quality to the food you share.

Preparing your own food can change the nature of the kitchen. Allow the kitchen to cheerfully reflect the vital changes you are making. Add small area rugs. Replace utility chairs with comfortable wooden ones, and put up more pictures and posters. Add color with plants, fresh and dried flowers and herbs, glass canisters, wooden cutting boards, and wicker baskets for fruits and vegetables. Grow herbs on your window sills, or sprouts on counter tops. The kitchen will become a more meaningful place, a more enchanting center where food is celebrated.

*A*nd *she had never forgotten that, if you drink much from a bottle marked "poison," it is almost certain to disagree with you, sooner or later.*

Lewis Carroll
Alice in Wonderland

I have said that one key to a lifetime diet is to become knowledgeable about the quality of foods, that is their nutritional value. I do not mean to suggest that you need to study definitive texts on the subject; on the other hand, there is a need to be informed about fundamentals, some of which I have covered in the preceding section. Ridding your diet of empty calories and poor-quality food items puts you on the right road. Generally speaking, high-quality food items are those that combine in meals that supply complete protein, vitamins, minerals, and essential fats along with their carbohydrates.

ATTRACTIVE ALTERNATIVES

Whenever possible, eat plenty of fresh vegetables, raw or lightly cooked. Eat raw and dried fruits, and fresh sprouts such as mung bean and alfalfa. Savor hearty dishes containing whole grains and legumes such as beans, peas, and lentils in combination. Seeds such as sunflower and unhulled sesame will add nutrition. Enjoy nuts and nut butters in moderation. A dish containing fish, eggs, or a dairy food such as milk, cheese or yogurt (with most of the butter fat removed) may be consumed once a day at first. Later you may wish to eat these foods less often, perhaps three or four times a week. It would be wise to break the habit of drinking excessive amounts of milk.

Some people consider shellfish "the scavengers of the ocean." In any case, shellfish should be eaten in moderation because of its cholesterol. Some believe that it is wrong to butcher mammals and eat their flesh, while others contend that meat contains potentially toxic additives that packers and processors use to "improve" its qualities. In recent years the plight of the calf and lamb has become especially horrendous. The extent to which such allegations are true or not is but one issue. Another is that it is unwise to eat meat. We have been conditioned to believe that we are carnivores by nature. This is not true. Studies have shown that human beings are basically vegetarians and, as such, we should be eating a wide variety of plant foods and decreasing our intake of animal foods. Meat, especially beef, is a digestive burden. As noted earlier, it is important to cut back on fat consumption, and fat is contained in even the leanest cuts. The fact that meat is also expensive ought not to be overlooked. Perhaps the best reason to avoid it is that as a food for those interested in alert life and good health, meat is simply unnecessary. Complete protein such as it provides is readily available elsewhere, and once meat is removed from your diet it becomes easier to maintain lighter eating habits.

I found that as my awareness of consumption changed my body did not need meat. I learned to get excellent protein from fish, a minimum intake of eggs, cheese and yogurt, and combinations of grains and legumes. I also discovered that tofu is a marvelous meat substitute. Meat was heavy and too much energy seemed wasted on digestion. Once I quit eating meat I could hardly enjoy it again; it had an unpleasant odor and taste. Whether or not you choose to exclude meat from your own lifetime diet, I urge you in the beginning to make an effort to cut back the amount you consume. Try a few days, or better yet, two or three successive weeks without it. Feel the difference this makes in you and your body.

Today we are fortunate that sounder advice regarding diet and consumption is available. At the same time, we find our diet subjected to an increased advertising assault from giant producers and processors. In an effort to distract us from the serious problems of preservatives, additives, and carcinogenics, they claim "natural" products that also provide us with convenience. Evidence of this can be found in health-food stores as well as the supermarkets. It is safe to say that convenience has become a contemporary curse, for there comes a point at which the fundamental action or acts of life should not be, indeed, cannot be reduced. Carefully selected produce and groceries, and long evenings spent slowly preparing and enjoying a homemade meal, are all too often aborted because dazzling deli or gourmet counters offer prepared food for "just a few pennies more." Such substitution can be a travesty that disrupts the precious rhythm of time and experience. It is as bad as substituting the automatically-dialed phone call and answering machine message for the rich communication that only the handwritten letter can convey.

In the early 1970s the writing of Frances Moore Lappe and Ellen Buchman Ewald was instrumental in revealing an intelligent alternative to the problems of consumption. In *Diet for a Small Planet*, Lappe gave examples of protein complementarity, which is "the combination, in proper proportions, of non-meat foods that produce high-grade protein nutrition equivalent to—or better than—meat proteins." She made it clear that plant protein was in no way inferior to animal protein, and that plant foods were superior to meat by virtue of the vitamins and minerals they contain and their virtual absence of fat. For example, a dish combining one-and-a-half cups of beans or peas with four cups of brown rice contains usable protein equivalent to nineteen ounces of steak. The tastiness and savoriness of such dishes is enhanced by herbs and vegetables. Lappe's work on protein complementarity was inspired by Ewald and grew into *Recipes for a Small Planet*, which included hundreds of easy recipes that combined grains, legumes, seeds, and dairy products into dishes that contain complete proteins as well as abundant vitamins and minerals. Testament to the validity of Ewald and Lappe's effort is the fact that their work is still emulated and their books are still in print.

Whether we call them "health foods", "holistic" or "natural," dramatic change has occurred in what we eat and why. Today we are the beneficiaries of a continual bounty of new information and styles of consumption that improve our lives. The work of Mollie Katzen has shown that a good diet does not have to conflict with a lifestyle that is active and seeking personal growth. In *The Moose-wood Cookbook* and her more recent *Still Life with Menu*, Katzen has detailed recipes and marvelously styled instructions that prove that fine food can be prepared ahead of time or in minimal time, allowing you to relax and enjoy your meals when you get home from work.

II.

However you improve your consumption, it is important to vary the foods you eat. This is an established principle of a sound diet, yet it bears repeating because people often get stuck on a small number of favorite dishes.

Potatoes are a wonderful food and can be prepared in countless ways. Instead of eating potatoes four or five times a week, however, try the tuber called Jerusalem artichoke which is similar in texture but deliciously different in taste. Or enjoy sopping up the juices of your entree with fresh, hot, whole-grain biscuits, or egg noodles made with pastry-grade whole-wheat flour. Avoid fried potatoes, especially French fried, which are deep-fat cooked. Cook potatoes, skins and all, after you have scrubbed them thoroughly; the skins also contain valuable nutrients.

Diversifying your diet is essential. Nutritionists agree that the body requires more than forty nutrients to sustain a high level of health. It is reasonable to expect that the more varied your choice of whole foods, the more likely these vital nutrients will be obtained.

Remember to drink water—lots of water—each day and, as much as possible, be aware of the source of that water. For variety drink more vegetable and fruit juices, and herbal teas for relaxing refreshment and to complement your meals.

Experts say that one should drink eight glasses or two quarts of water per day.

I like to get some of this amount mixed half and half with a fruit or vegetable juice. If you have any doubts about the purity of your tap water, investigate the variety of purification devices and, meanwhile, buy natural spring water for drinking and cooking as well as to prepare tea. As for other liquids available in the marketplace these days, be suspicious of soft drinks of all kinds! Most carbonated drinks ought to be labeled with a skull and crossbones. Between the sugar or sugar substitute, the sodium, the coal-tar dyes and all the other harmful additives, these concoctions might be useful as drain-cleaners and rust removers, but they are unfit for human consumption. Of alcoholic drinks, a lifetime diet should allow only occasional wine, beer or light drink. Alcohol can provide a beneficial balance to any diet and a wondrous magic to life as well—but in moderate amounts.

As your consumption changes it is important to be alert to your changing tastes. Early on I began to react negatively to coffee. It seemed thick, oily, and acidic and left an aftertaste and odor in my mouth. These sensations were so disagreeable that I came to the conclusion the oil and acidity in coffee were more detrimental than the caffeine. Fortunately I was able to give up coffee. Soon after, reacting to the caffeine and tannic acid in black teas, I began to curb that habit as well. However, I feel both may be enjoyed in moderate amounts. An alternative to drinking coffee and "hard" tea is to explore the myriad choices of herbal teas. Sipped alone, or slightly sweetened with honey, they are endowed with soothing, rejuvenating qualities. The magical healing power of herbs is a gift of nature that still tends to be ignored. It is a blessing that herbal teas are available in grocery as well as health-food stores. Once you have acquired a taste for herbal teas you will become averse to the harsh taste for coffee and black tea.

As I have pointed out, the key to the lifetime diet is to prepare food yourself. The physical touch—the selection and preparation of what you eat—is probably as important as the foodstuff. Preparation allows you to remove yourself from all other activity, to think about and handle what you will be putting into your body. The mind and hand participate in combining foods into appealing and wholly satisfying dishes. In personal preparation of foods, something of you goes into them and their nourishment is enhanced by your attentiveness. Food is life, and through a powerful, active awareness of food you learn to treat life with new respect. Remember, foods should be cooked only long enough to make them digestible. Learn to use a wok. When stir-frying, cut vegetables into bite-size pieces. A pressure cooker is best for cooking whole grains. The multi-purpose juicer and food mill is a must for preparing fresh vegetables, fruit juices, and grinding grains into meals and flour.

Personally, as the years go by, I lean more and more toward vegetarianism because I love the lightness of fruits and vegetables and my body has lost the habit of heavy food. When I can manage it—as it needs about three or four hours—baking breads or rolls of various whole grains gives me immense satisfaction. It is simple to freeze half of the dough to be baked another day. With other dishes that lend themselves to freezing, I prepare twice as much as I need and freeze the rest for a meal the following week. Economy and efficiency are realized in this way, and proper storage and timely defrosting insures that little or nothing is lost in nourishment or taste.

Somewhere in the conflicting impulses and urges that arise into our awareness when we think of eating is the data which we need to guide us to the food that our bodies require. These internal indicators have to be patiently retrained, however. What is often referred to as hunger, for example, is not really hunger at all but the socially or psychologically conditioned urge to eat. One has to filter out all the other connections involved with food, tuning in to the correct signals and tuning out the static.

Rudolph Ballentine, M.D.
Diet and Nutrition

III.

Sober consideration of consumption leads us to a second major area of diet: eating habits and how much to eat. In America, generally speaking, our lives are plagued by an overindulgence in food. The reasons are numerous, complex and often unconscious, but the main reason is that feeling "full" is imagined relief from practically everything that ails us. Too often eating becomes an attack on boredom and frustration, a reward for the trials of life, or an act of aggression, which gets repeated again and again with dreadful results. Moreover, snacking has been turned into a national tradition, heavily promoted by insidious advertising that pushes junk food and drink with the vile insistence on the great fun of what has become collective gluttony.

Chances are that the average person reading this book might cut out 20%, even 30% of what she or he eats and still be furnishing the body with enough nutrients, as well as restoring a zestful appetite. To develop a sense of what and what not to eat, and how much to eat, you need removal. You need to step back and then step back again to gain a realistic perspective. Only then will the practicality of a basic principle of a lifetime diet become clear: when in doubt, don't! Don't snack or indulge. Never fear to skip a meal. Eat wisely at regular mealtimes. Learn to fast. Free the self from the dominations of appetite.

Freedom from old habits will strengthen you with a new command of yourself. If your health is basically good and your diet consists of wholesome foods and balanced meals, there is nothing nutritionally unsound about occasionally eating two, even one meal a day, or restricting consumption to fourteen or sixteen meals a week with a day or two of reasonable fasting every month. The benefits of regular, sensible fasting are incredible. Fasting is a control over consumption that relieves and stills the digestive system and provides a lightness of body and spirit. The tyranny of food consumption is a wall against individual awareness and the expansion of consciousness. The average person's eating habits are formed under a commercial totalitarianism that actually impedes the development and maintenance of a truly healthy body and blocks the freedom of the full utilization of that body.

We have been reduced. We have made fetishes out of expedience and convenience. Consider the claims of fast-food chains, of sugared breakfast cereals, unnatural "orange drink." Consider the perfidious insistence that to constantly drink milk is good for you. Many health experts feel this is quite untrue. Reject the ritualistic call for the consumption of "three squares a day!" Compare this to the glossy, grossly expensive commercials that inevitably follow homey skits extolling antacids and other stomach remedies—genteel pitches aimed at "hemorrhoid sufferers" and those "with occasional irregularity." The hundreds of millions of dollars spent on such advertising would seem to admit to a national constipation. Match these considerations with the seemingly patriotic—idiotic—gluing and cleaning of dentures. These mindless vignettes have become a staple of prime-time television. Were it not sad, it would be hilarious that a nation is so manipulated into false mystiques of overeating and wrongful eating, then sold products to undo the mischief suffered by the body.

Since there is no money to be made from it, a conspiracy of silence seems to reign in the media over the subject of sensible eating and the development of fasting habits. Having few supports for such a project, even people who know better shamelessly procrastinate.

"I can't fast because of my schedule!"

"I could lose weight any time . . . if I wanted to."

Endless statements like these ring false and fail to admit the addictive element of food. Now, at the end of the twentieth century, overweight America is an international scandal. We seem obsessed with gorging ourselves and are constantly anxious about cleaning and eliminating the harried systems of our bodies that process what we eat. Does one eat to live or live to eat? Life priorities are confused if one spends too much time and energy on food. This confusion numbs the senses and anesthetizes the mind, keeping us from coping with the real problems and true challenges of human existence. Overeating and all its paraphernalia are thieves of health which leave our ailing bodies and preoccupied minds no time or energy to think for freeing ourselves. We need to see that there is a greater reality in being free.

Fasting is an excellent tool.

Fasting is a way to cleanse the body's digestive and elimination systems and to purify all the senses. We shall begin to see it as a means of unburdening the body to allow us a greater awareness. Fasting quiets the mind and brings us back to ourselves so that we are better able to contemplate and act on the changes we instinctively desire.

FASTING

Fasting should be treated religiously. It is best to begin with an eight- or ten-hour fast during the day. For example, only one or two meals, perhaps abstaining from lunch and breaking the fast with a light meal toward evening. Or you may wish to abstain from breakfast and have one midday meal. Work up to the point where you eat only one meal, settling for juice or water for the others. Go gradually until your body becomes used to the changes and the lack of reward that eating provides. Never push your body or shock it into a long fast. Always prepare. Always relax. The fast is a treatment for the mind as well as the body.

When you feel ready to fast for a 24- or 36-hour period, try to be alone and remain quiet. Enjoy a day of silence. Conversation drains energy. Some people might understand and respect the time you are devoting to yourself, but do not risk interruption. Unplug the telephone. Treat yourself to calm removal and relaxation. By fasting you are caring for yourself by purifying your body and training yourself to eat less. Enjoy the quiet and reverie. Play soothing music or spend time reading. Write or paint or even dance to the music, letting your body flow in the rhythm of a dance of its own. Do nothing laborious. Focus on yourself and the changes you may feel in your body. Your senses will be heightened and, after the hunger pangs have receded—and they always do recede—you will experience a new clarity that will beckon you again and again to a private world about which you knew so little.

When you break a fast do it with gentle control. Eat lightly, perhaps a nourishing soup or a melon, apple or pear. Later, you may have a meal, but be aware of how much your stomach has shrunk. Above all, watch what you eat. Avoid sugar or spiced food. Chew slowly and eat less. As you come off a fast dwell on the matter of nutrition and consumption. You will be lighter, more energetic, and more ready to explore your feelings. You will have escaped the intoxication and lethargy caused by food. You will have begun to revolt against the tyrannies.

At the beginning of this chapter I used the phrase "body wisdom" and spoke of the need to intuit the body's nutritional requirements. Although this seems to be a somewhat mysterious faculty, it is acknowledged by those who study human nutrition. The eminent biochemist Roger J. Williams has written that "one of the regulatory mechanisms or 'wisdoms' of the body is that we eat when we are hungry and stop when we have had enough . . . It seems probable that individual nutritional needs are met to a degree by the self-selection of foods. This is particularly so when the selection involves only wholesome foods . . ." Williams, Rudolph Ballentine and my late mother agree, however, that for most people in America today this intuition has been numbed by years of wrongful eating habits. We confuse what we hunger for with what we desire to eat and, as a consequence, the body does not get what it needs. It is fed what we desire. The guidelines of a lifetime diet point the way out of this tyranny. *A lifetime diet should be incorporated systematically, slowly and thoughtfully. Bear in mind that these are guidelines only and not a detailed set of instructions, use them to inspire your personal investigations of your individual nutritional requirements.* As you gradually progress in learning the truth about foods and apply this learning, you can expect to hear from and be aided by the intuitive wisdom of your body. The careful and considered use of the tool of fasting is the key to help along the way.

Sensible eating concerns what and how much as well as the manner in which food is eaten. Many people habitually hurry through their meals. If there is not enough time to sit down and eat at a pace that respects both the food and the diner, I suggest that the time is better spent not eating at all. A short walk or a brief meditation would be healthier. Even when there is time to enjoy a leisurely meal, many tend to hurry. The development of slower eating habits is imperative. It creates instant mindfulness of eating. Not only is it beneficial to the digestion, but thorough chewing slows down the food intake and allows you the opportunity to taste and relish the meal. By this means alone it is possible to eat less without feeling a sense of deprivation.

Let a calm atmosphere reign over your dining area. Mealtime should be a period of appreciation, praise, and gratitude for the food that sustains our life and the people who have brought the food to our table. The radio or stereo may furnish suitable background music but turn off the television. Awareness of the food itself should be paramount. When dining with family or friends, try not to discuss personal problems or bring up any heavy topic of conversation. Low voices and pleasant talk lend the proper ambience to dining in the company of others. These should be happy, meaningful moments, a time when you are gathered in an atmosphere of warmth, nourishment, and love.

IV.

Once you have established a new nutrition and are eating less, extend your lifetime diet to include regulation of everything that goes into your mouth. All your improvements could be ruined by the use of tobacco or ill-considered use of alcohol. I shall return to these items in Chapter Five, where other types of consumption affecting consciousness are considered.

The stages of change that culminate in a lifetime diet may be seen as a gradual process of purifying the body and mind. The process is not unlike a journey up a mountain. At the peak is a purity that releases new energy and helps rid life of disease and the needless debility of premature aging. To knowledgeably control everything you put into your mouth lowers the risk of contaminating your body with chemicals, additives, and fraudulent foods. In the beginning, at the base of the mountain, you eat poorly. A step up, and you free yourself from devitalized and junk foods. Higher, you are free of commercially prepared food products. You have all but stopped drinking coffee and are discovering the pleasure of herbal teas. You do not use tobacco and moderate your consumption of wine and beer. When you rid your diet of red meat you are higher, and higher still when you rarely ever eat flesh. At the summit, you eat only natural foods and fast regularly. You have a communion with preparing what you eat. You have risen above the ordinary plagues of life.

For myself, as I have mentioned, scaling the mountain was a continuing project that called forth and simultaneously replenished discipline and determination. Through the years, as I slowly and haltingly shed the habit of using white flour, sugar, red meat, coffee, tobacco, and alcohol, I began to enjoy more abundant energy. Cooking for myself, I became free from other tyrannies and required less sleep, gaining more time to explore my inner self—the strange friend it took so long to find. As I opened this exploration my awareness increased still more. This new sense of my life—the one that came from within—needed direction, and I was ready for and capable of greater expectations.

4.

Relaxation and Meditation

What is my motive for meditation? I want to die—to die out of my present state and discover new aspects of me that are evolving. I do not want to hinder this growth or become stagnant . . . meditation offers a bridge to walk consciously from one stage of growth to the next.

Jack Schwarz
Voluntary Controls

I.

A personalized exercise program that is appealing and vitalizing combined with a lifetime plan of food consumption that furnishes a wholesome diet cannot help but produce a healthy, energized body and mind. One way or another many people accomplish this much. To go no farther would be regrettable, yet it seems that few people realize that the destination they seek lies beyond the accomplishments of exercise and diet.

Improving health and social functioning by instilling a regime of beneficial exercise and diet is necessary, but in and of themselves not sufficient to develop one's full potential for expanding consciousness, the aim of the truly concerned individual. The next step in the journey is back to the self, the ultimate migration: To master one's own mind. The Indian yoga master Swami Rama maintains that all of the body is in the mind but not all of the mind is in the body. As you increase awareness and vitality of your psychosomatic self you are inevitably led to consideration of your psycho-spiritual self. This chapter deals with the difficult challenge of governing the mind, and the final step of connecting daily living with the spirit. Meditation is the key.

I suggest that as you continue to develop a program of self-transformation you establish disciplines of the body before taking up meditation, the mental discipline. I believe this is preferable for most people. Many begin with meditation, perhaps because they feel no need to improve their physical condition. People who truly have no such need are quite rare, however, and the chances are great that were you to ignore exercise and consumption control and begin meditating regularly you would be led back to diet and exercise. The practice of learning to control your attention, for that is what meditation boils down to, is a very demanding one that calls for every advantage you can bring to it.

In meditation we gather and focus the energy derived from exercise and consumption control, and thereby achieve what seems impossible in modern life. We meditate to center ourselves. We meditate to create distance from the chaotic psychological and environmental conditions in which we live. Although this is not its primary goal, meditation does help to develop awareness of what is required to better steer through times of confusion or pain. Through this development we succeed in gaining control of our destinies. Meditation centers one on an inner essence whose genius is mastery of all that is petty and destructive in life so that one may move toward what is grand and constructive.

THE SILENT ADVANTAGE

Meditation permits you to experience the truth that your body and mind are informed by, and infused with, the essence called spirit.

Meditation is the means that allows this truth to emerge into awareness, thereby enabling one to function as a whole person whose body, mind, and spirit abide in harmony and balance under all circumstances.

This in turn refines awareness and expands consciousness. Meditation opens you to greater realities . . . rewarding realms that await exploration.

There is a limitless potential to be discovered and enjoyed.

By practicing meditation you learn to still the eternal (some say infernal) monologue inside your head; then, in the stillness you become aware of a certain presence. It is the self within whose existence had been buried by the noise and combustion of daily concern that can ruinously hinder ordinary life. Your spiritual nature has always been there although it was denied recognition. Meditation enables you to heal the division of your totality.

Before saying more about this division, its origin and consequences, I need to point out the important, practical reason to meditate that cannot be overlooked by anyone. It is the antidote to the harmful effects of stress. Psycho-social stress is a major contributing factor in the development of high blood pressure and heart disease, cancer, arthritis, and many other so-called "afflictions of civilization." In Kenneth Pelletier's *Mind as Healer, Mind as Slayer*, we learn that "too many people are only vaguely aware of the cost of stress." In the lives we lead stress is inevitable. To live the lives we choose stress cannot be avoided altogether, but it is of the utmost importance that extremes of stress be identified and controlled by *true* relaxation. Meditation is a superlative way to "unstress," to calm and restore to normal functioning those vital systems of your body that automatically raise alarms when presented with psycho-social stresses.

The illusory securities sought through the daily pursuit of love and sex, money and power, and threatened by the uncertainties of materialism and professionalism, can be seen for what they are through meditation. Too much of daily life today produces conflict, ambiguity, frustration, and discontent. Trying to soothe frayed nerves with sugar, alcohol, Valium, or some other device produces a deadly backlash. Escape into the mindless entertainments of television or ill-considered movies offers no solution at all. Partaking in outdoor recreation or social activities may provide some degree of stress relief but can never supply what is truly needed. Deeply restorative relaxation is essential to one's well-being, and meditation is the best way to accomplish this vital task. In *Mind as Healer, Mind as Slayer*, Kenneth Pelletier reviewed the scientific evidence on the subject and concluded as follows:

> The preliminary research . . . indicates that the conscientious practice of meditation increases autonomic stability, aids in the habituation to repeated stresses, and produces a state of relaxation deeper in some respects than that induced during sleep. In addition, the characteristic physiological pattern of a person during meditation is virtually opposite to that of a neurophysiological stress pattern. These effects of the meditation can carry over and extend into the post-meditation stage of daily activity. These studies imply that regular meditation can be an effective means of stress alleviation.

Yet this, no more than insight into the conditions that harry us, is not the goal of meditation either. What the legions of modern medical science have begun to glimpse the poet Thoreau fully grasped a hundred years ago when he wrote, "Health requires this relaxation, this aimless life. This life in the present."

I believe it is useful to try to understand how our spiritual nature came to be submerged, cut off, and divided from awareness. To cope successfully with the demands of modern life our minds have been trained to work within boundaries. This categorization begins in early childhood and grows more complex with age. The result is that we become exclusively committed to a linear, rational, and manipulative mode of thinking. This aspect of mind, the intellect, with its powers of reasoning and ability to deal with objects and relationships in space and time, enables us to get on in the world. It is geared to the conditions of social necessity and is essential to material survival. But it is, nevertheless, only one aspect of mind. Other aspects—namely intuitive and spiritual modes of apprehending reality—are not seen as essential to social or material functioning. Consequently, for the most part they are left undeveloped. According to ancient Eastern tradition, most of us are "asleep." It is as if we have never explored the entire mansion of the mind, as if we lived in only a few rooms, unconscious of the possibilities of other rooms, other worlds, oblivious to the magnificence of the whole. Our conditioned minds, the few rooms we know so well, reveal only very limited areas of reality. To remain asleep, ignorant of other worlds, of the whole, is to remain unfulfilled, living the meager, partial life that such conditioning produces.

One of the benefits of modern, New Age interest has been a growing awareness of this division, increased recognition that intuitive and spiritual modes are neither unnatural nor unhealthy. Despite criticism of much New Age activity, most contemporary authorities recognize that there can be no true contentment or lasting satisfaction so long as a division between our mundane and spiritual selves prevails. Indeed, to ignore this division can only lead to lethargy, frustration, and despair in which we suspect we are only half-alive, only partially grown.

The objective conditioning of the rational mind is necessary for survival in the material world, but merely to survive is not to live a fully human life! *There is no mystery to materialism, but there is to human existence.* Meditation illuminates the mystery and reveals the enigma. Best of all, meditation is free. It can be accomplished by anyone willing to practice. Alone, or with others, it is the perfect approach to fulfilling that deep desire for something other, something more. No deprogramming is necessary. The tools are relaxation and personal discipline. No matter who you are or where you are, you can learn to use meditation to abolish division, to enter into and enjoy your full estate of living consciousness.

In *the rush to capture the market of would-be meditators, some organizations have spread distortions about meditation. The notion, for example, that only one kind of meditation can change one for the better, while others cannot, masks the basic sameness of all meditation techniques.*

Daniel Goleman
*The Varieties of the Meditative
Experience*

II.

What is meditation? Even as we begin the 1990s, when the practice and popularity of meditation has soared, the question still has many answers. Often meditation is confused with prayer or contemplation. A simple way of differentiating is to see that prayer and contemplation are objective, whereas meditation is totally non-objective. In prayer one is usually following a form, invoking some deity or power beyond the ordinary self, in order to ask help or express gratitude. In contemplation, attention dwells on an object; we contemplate a problem, or a lover, a financial situation, perhaps the countryside, a mountain, or flowers. Prayer and contemplation can be rich and helpful in focusing thoughts or conditions, but they are not meditation.

Meditation is non-objective. Your attention has no focus beyond the present moment. One abides in a "choiceless awareness," to use Krishnamurti's words. The need to retrain attention to this end, according to Goleman, "is the single invariant ingredient in the recipe for altering consciousness of every meditation system." We need to transcend all thought and mental impression, withdraw attention from the chatter of mind so that all the worries and cares as well as the victories and glories of ego dissolve. It is rather like turning off the furnace, shutting down all the heat of human desire and involvement. By ceasing to pay attention to ego concerns you cause them to fade and extinguish. You have turned off the big switch to the world—all of glasnost, China, The Middle East, and world hunger—to your country, your home, your workplace, to all the friends, lovers and creditors in your life. You forget those who pollute the world and those striving to preserve its precious resources. As you switch off the television and the picture fades and the image is lost, so you may do with the self through meditation. For a time you are lost to the mundane world and enter a state of wondrous comfort and removal. *This is the point where the continuum of stress is severed.*

Your mind may bathe in colors you have never envisioned; images never before seen may appear. You may experience sensations of floating or soaring. Conversely, you may feel physical discomfort. Your foot falls asleep and begins to prickle, your nose itches and wants scratching, your back aches or your stomach rumbles with hunger. All these experiences too, whether painful, irritating, delightful or scary, are impermanent and will pass away as you continue to withhold attention from them. Remember that, unlike contemplation or prayer, meditation has no object. Eventually, if you persist and your zeal matches in intensity the purity of your endeavor, you become aware of a limitless, totally alive and dynamic void. There arises with clarity the wordless conviction that you are one with this infinitude. It is at this moment that meditation creates the spiritual connection. That which you become aware of as all encompassing is your inner essence, a spiritual you, the you that links with and is not different from eternal life.

This knowledge confirms a center that is love and, if you open to it, love will fill your being. Love, the highest state of being, is what is positive in life and no matter who or where we are, no matter what age, we hunger for it. It is a mystical necessity, this link with the spiritual. We connect body, mind, and spirit and in this state of love are united with others who are so connected.

Access to that conviction of who you are does not belong to a chosen few or a particular sect. It is not exclusive to religions or organizations but freely open to all who know how to seek it. Meditation has no certified origin. The tradition reaches into the West as well as the East. It was ancient when history began. There is no obligation to join or believe in anything. It is a natural gift, an innate ability each individual has, an ability that will eventually transport you toward the heights of greater consciousness.

MINDFULNESS

There is no one approved method of meditation. No single text could encompass the entire magnitude of meditation or, for that matter, consciousness. If you feel the need to receive instruction, to join a meditation class or attend a seminar or workshop, by all means do so. The best you can do with such instruction is to discern and assimilate the basic techniques as practiced by meditation masters. But the concerned individual should be wary of shortcuts as well as disciplines and dogmatic systems. Meditation practiced in a religious context or embedded within a quasi-scientific system usually requires an emotional allegiance that is unnecessary.

The extent to which awareness and consciousness have been merchandised in the past decade is regrettable, for they are free and as much a birthright as breathing. However, this should not dissuade you from investigating means and methods because, as with breathing, you can learn from those who have devoted many years of study to the subject. But whoever your teachers are and whatever method you begin with, you will eventually discover you have a spiritual teacher inside you who will lovingly guide if you will only listen and trust. For most people, the notion of an external guru is a seductive myth, yet a true master is one who puts you in touch with yourself, opens you to yourself and to the teacher within you. Beyond that, with rare exception, the role of pupil to master, of servant to saint, can be dangerous. It can be a cruel game that ensnares you in another's powerful ego that preys on innocence and ignorance.

Trust in yourself.

Learn and discover a method best suited to your personality and environment and your aims in life. A sincere desire to meditate and to understand the value of centering will produce this method.

"**H**ow can you go on talking so quietly, head downwards? . . . "

"What does it matter where my body happens to be?" he said, "My mind goes on working all the same."

Lewis Carroll
Through the Looking Glass

The basic requirements for meditation concern your body and the environment. Posture is important for it must be coordinated with breathing. The development of right posture frees the body. In seated meditation the upper body needs to be relaxed but not saggingly so, the back erect but not rigid, while the lower body provides a solid, stable base. Strength and awareness are required to hold the torso and head upright. Never strain. Do not suck in the belly military-style. The natural curve of your lower spine should be respected. Keep your chin tucked in and your ears in line with your shoulders and hips. This positioning aligns and keeps open the thorax and chest for maximum ease of breathing. Focus on keeping your shoulders in the same plane as your hips and the whole weight of your head centered over, and balanced on top of, the spine.

You may sit comfortably on an armless chair with a firmly cushioned seat, using the forward third or so to support your buttocks and placing your feet flat on the floor. Or you may sit on the floor, using the forward third of a fairly firm cushion to support your buttocks. In either position, relax your shoulders and arms and place your hands comfortably on your lap. Always remember to keep the back and head erect. Whichever position you choose, whether on a chair or on the floor, always take a few moments to center yourself so that you are perfectly stable and at ease and not inclined to move. The prime requisite of meditation is to remain still.

You may wish to vary seated meditation postures with the "corpse" pose, described in the exercise chapter, in which you lie flat on the floor. It should be noted that the problem of falling asleep arises when using this pose for meditation. Nevertheless, many claim that the position has an advantage in that without the strain of support the body enjoys the greatest level of tension reduction.

With reference to sitting on the floor, the question arises: what to do with the legs? The classic solution is called the lotus pose with right foot atop left thigh, heel against groin and left foot atop right thigh, heel against groin, and knees on the floor. Here the hands are composed in the classic Zen manner generally called the cosmic mudra. Resting the hands against the lower belly, place the palms upwards, left on top of the right, with thumbtips touching. This positioning of the hands can be an aid in concentration as well. Should the thumbs sag during meditation, it would be a clear indication of a loss of alertness.

The lotus pose should not be forced. Unless one has been sitting this way from adolescence, say, when physical growth is virtually complete yet the bones, muscles and tendons are still supple and highly educable, very few people, whether Asian or Western, can get into this position much less be comfortable in it for any length of time. It is considered the ultimate posture for meditation because it provides the most stable base. You might be more comfortable with the half-lotus which requires less agility. This is similar to the lotus pose except you tuck the right foot under the left thigh, the left foot on top of the right thigh with both knees resting on the floor. If one knee or the other is uncomfortable use a thin cushion to support it. You may want to invest in some equipment to aid your posture in the lotus or half-lotus position. I recommend a zafu, a round cushion, which you can place atop a semi-thick, rectangular mat, or small rug. Choose a cushion with a comfortable firmness. If you experiment with the lotus or half-lotus pose, move gently! If they prove too difficult, abandon them.

An alternative is the so-called Burmese positioning in which legs are folded parallel to one another, knees resting on the floor. In this pose you can sit on a wooden meditation bench, an angled support that fits beneath the thighs. It provides the perfect answer for the elderly or those suffering from knee trouble.

If any of these positions work for you, fine, but most people, especially in the beginning, should simply sit in whatever folded-legs manner is natural and comfortable for them. Here are a few exercises that will help you stretch and strengthen the leg muscles used in sitting on the floor:

> Sit on the floor. Bring the soles of your feet together. Take hold of your toes with your hands and gently pull your feet toward you. Using your elbows or hands, push your knees down toward the ground—pull-push, pull-push— for a minute or more.

Sit on the floor and put your legs out straight in front of you. Place your right foot on the thigh above your left knee. Use your right hand to work your knee up and down. After a minute or so, reverse your position and do the same with the other knee.

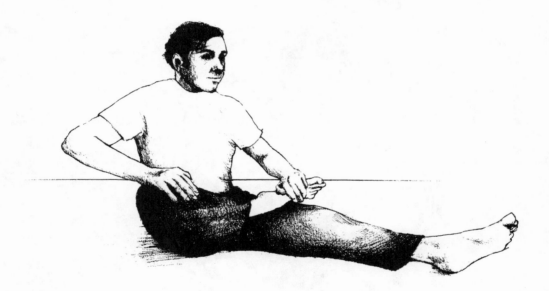

Sit on the floor. With legs out straight in front of you, place the sole of your right foot against the left thigh. Use your right hand to work your knee up and down; after a minute or so, reverse your position and do the same with the other knee.

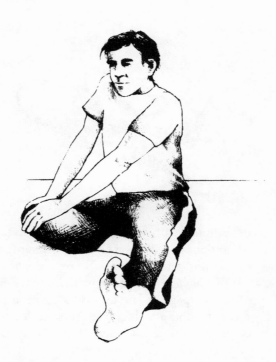

The meditation posture I prefer is to sit on the floor with a cushion tucked comfortably underneath me. My legs are bent toward the crotch, the soles of my feet turned upward and one heel resting on top of the other. The cushion is adjusted so that my knees rest on the floor with ease and my back is straight.

You may want to experiment with various alternatives to find the best posture according to your height and physical proportions. Be tolerant, gentle, and patient with yourself. Above all, do not get caught up in any ideas about the "right" way to sit. Many attach a certain *hauteur* to sitting in the classic manner but this has nothing to do with meditation, per se. The aim is to position the upper body and head so that they are erect, to find a stable base, then to forget the body. This is why it is best not to meditate until at least one or two hours after eating. This is why you wear light, loose clothing or, if the room is warm enough, perhaps no clothing at all. Secured by complete privacy the rewards of a nude or semi-nude meditation can be incredible. I recommend beginning with a basic honesty by baring the body. We spend most of our lives covered or armed by garments and tend to forget that within those layers of fabric and fashion there is a warm, pulsating body. Meditating in the nude makes you that much more aware of your whole physical reality.

It is believed that the ideal time to meditate is in the early hours of the morning. On arising, go for a brisk walk or a jog. Bathe or shower to refresh yourself and, in those hours before the din of the material world begins, meditate. This might mean getting up earlier, but an established program should help. One of the changes brought by developing awareness is that you end each day before midnight. This is not always possible, but do so whenever you can in order to take advantage of the magic of early morning. Not enough can be said for the quiet hours between 4 AM and 7 AM. From a practical standpoint they offer more removal than any other time of day, but they also have qualities which are not apparent until experienced. In the world around you less traffic is running, less electricity is being used, phones are silent, fewer people are about. Above all, the sky and the air are different. In most cities these are the only hours it is possible to hear birds singing.

At first it may be difficult to establish and maintain this routine, but once you begin you will not want to change. Conversely, some may get into it easily and enthusiastically but find their resolve to carry on begin to wane. A moderate degree of enthusiasm is certainly desirable, but it is unwise to get excited about beginning a meditation habit. Remember, like the final diet, meditation is a permanent habit you wish to establish. Slow but sure is the course; steadiness and resolution are the most helpful attitudes. Before long—probably within days or a few weeks—the first rewards will amply repay your effort. One of the things you will notice is that since meditating is rejuvenating you will have greater patience and require less sleep. It will become easier to master the day before it begins.

If you are unable to meditate in the morning, find another time in the day. Before bedtime is fine, providing you are not too tired and have not eaten for two hours or so. Many choose to meditate after work, before dinner. Again, if possible, refresh yourself by bathing or showering beforehand and do a few minutes of gentle stretching to release the tensions of the day. Then, meditate. Concentrate on how much better it feels to meditate and renew the energies of your being than to try and appease the stressed self with alcohol or television. Whatever hour of the day works best for you, try to keep to that time, for this will help establish the habit. Meditate every day, even if only for fifteen or twenty minutes. Have a clock or watch placed where you can see it without having to move. One-half to three-quarters of an hour would be best. If a daily routine seems too much in the beginning, meditate three days of the week, keeping to the same days if possible.

Choose a quiet room that is neither too dimly lit, which might foster dozing off, nor too bright, neither too warm, or too cool. Master meditators do not need such arrangements. In India yogis can sit in the middle of Calcutta traffic and meditate, but as a beginner living in the Western world you will need to eliminate or minimize distractions.

Silence the telephone.

Close the door.

Many can establish a time and place in the office for meditation. Years ago, I knew a calm, kind director of an import and export firm. Every day, a half-hour before his luncheon, he hung a "Do Not Disturb" sign on his door and instructed no calls be put through to him. Knowing only this much, I often kidded him about his afternoon naps. Months later, he looked at me and smilingly shook his head.

"I'm doing something far better," he said. "I'm meditating."

At that time his reply made little impression on me. Although I continued to envy his unfailing kind manner and wondered how a man with his responsibility managed to remain so relaxed and in such good spirits, I went on for years without connecting his personality with his meditating.

Getting together with other people who meditate can be very supportive once you've mastered the necessary fundamentals. Group meditation itself can be very powerful. It is not unusual to meet at homes for an evening of meditation especially if an area is arranged with a proper regard for privacy, ventilation and lighting. Afterwards tea can be served or even a potluck dinner. Such meetings are not only rewarding but help strengthen the practice.

Once you learn, you can meditate anywhere—on a bus or an airplane, on a park bench or at a beach—but in the beginning it is important to begin in a quiet, personal place that is reserved for work on yourself. It is wise to create an environment for meditation that is inviting, a place that will gradually enhance your practice. If you are lucky enough to have a spare room make this into a meditation and exercise center. Few furnishings are required: a thick rug, a fairly hard cushion or, if you prefer, an armless chair. If your floor covering is not thick enough or you don't have a mat, fold a soft blanket or use a few large bath towels. Let this place be your personal retreat where, for an hour or so every day, you shut the world off and attend to the self. Ensure the room is well-ventilated, the lighting soft. Make it a small haven, a shelter for green plants and favorite prints or a painting you especially like. Use a small table as an altar for flowers. If you do not have a spare room, any area can be adapted and reserved solely for this purpose. Whether a room or an area, create a personally pleasing place. The soft sound of taped music can guide your removal. A scented candle or the subtle perfume of incense can change the air and purify the atmosphere. This is the place from which you will begin to journey, take a first step toward that precious essence that will change your life.

Emphasis is placed on atmosphere because so many elements of our modern environment are antagonistic to removal, let alone to the regular practice of meditation. Especially in the beginning, I believe it is important to set aside time and properly prepare the place as well as the self. No matter where my travels take me I try to create an ambience conducive to meditation. I improve the atmosphere of a hotel room in whatever way I can. It is marvelous what a prudently placed stick of incense can do after the room has been cleared of advertisements, telephone books, and those intrusive room-service order forms usually placed to catch your eye. I sweep these into a drawer and place the telephone out of sight under a bed pillow. There is little that can be done about the glass eye of the television set; I either drape a robe over it, or simply turn my back to it. I arrange some flowers from a nearby stand and softly play music on my portable tape player. Then I take a hot bath in this serene environment I have prepared, in which the lingering effects of the crowded, sometimes frantic, conditions of travel are dissipated. To complete my restoration and renewal, I sit and meditate.

III.

Breathing and Devices

Meditation is a cumulative blessing. It has numerous ways of reproducing its effects. Once begun, it spreads and develops as a source of incredible relaxation and renewed confidence in your ability to become all that you are. In order to take advantage of this it is best to learn how to facilitate the habit.

After you have established the appropriate posture and atmosphere, begin to incorporate the basic fundamentals of breathing and exercise. Use the alternate nostril breathing described earlier to relax and calm you. The neck rolls and the eye exercises will help release tension. The key to understanding and utilizing the breath is to close your eyes and breathe deeply . . . slowly fill the diaphragm and chest, slowly breathe out, allowing the chest and diaphragm to contract.

Always breathe in and out only through your nose.

Feel as if you are breathing from the pit of your belly, what is known as the hara, the true center of your being. As Westerners we tend to think of the heart as the center of our being. Observing the human body in its entirety, we see that this is not so. The belly is our natural center and when we bring our attention to it and inhale deeply from it, we connect to the very groundness of our being. Breathe in naturally, fully. Do not squeeze the nostrils when inhaling. Focus the effort for a few moments on breathing in a certain rhythm, inhaling to the count of eight, exhaling to the count of eight. In breathing in and out relax the shoulders and keep your back and head comfortably erect.

Nothing about breathing or meditation should be forced.

IMAGINARY MECHANICS

Keep your eyelids lowered, allowing your gaze to rest on the floor a bit in front of you. Attend solely to the breath.

There are two distinct tones as you breathe in and out. The yogis say the incoming breath sounds like sa and the outgoing like hum. In Sanskrit these sounds mean "Thou art That," but in the beginning do not dwell on meaning. Simply breathe and give each breath undivided attention.

You can learn from those who practice Zen meditation by simply counting the breath as you inhale and exhale. Inhale, then count one on the exhalation, two on the inhalation and so on until ten, going back to the count of 1 to 10 again and again.

Breath is the present moment flowing through you. It reveals that meditation has no past or future. The goal, if one may call it a goal, is to escort awareness into the timelessness of here-and-now.

Focusing your sole attention on the breath is far from easy. In the classic book *How to Meditate*, Lawrence Le Shan said it well: "The first shock of surprise comes when one realizes how undisciplined the mind really is: how it refuses to do the bidding of our will. After 15 minutes of attempting only to count our breaths and not be thinking of anything else, we realize that if our bodies were half as responsive to our will as our minds are, we would never get across the street alive."

The act of breathing is unique among physiological functions in that it may transpire without awareness yet it may also, with the merest effort of will directing attention, be brought to consciousness. Sustaining that effort without pause, however, is the rub. Attention keeps slipping away. Now you have it; now you don't. Keeping the focus requires infinite, second-by-second care. You will be amazed and perhaps disheartened to discover how little control you have over your attention. Persist. As Le Shan rightly pointed out, "The important thing about meditation is how hard and consistently you work on it, not how 'well' you do it." He tells a story about Saint Bernard of Clairvaux who, when asked about the successfulness of his lifetime meditation practices, replied, "Oh how rare the hour and how brief its duration!"

You will experience how difficult it is to withdraw all attention from the monologuing mind. Over and over again you will find you have to refocus on the two tones of breathing or counting the breath. Other difficulties will arise. Bringing your breathing into consciousness is not the same as consciously breathing. The latter means that you are controlling your breath and, except when you wish to practice certain techniques of special breathing, the intent is simply to witness the natural ebb and flow of breath, to let it be. Similarly, make no effort to suppress thoughts, for that would be self-defeating. When allowed to surface, thoughts will dissipate themselves. Tibetan Buddhist meditation master Chogyam Trungpa, in an excellent collection of his lectures entitled *Meditation in Action*, advised about the thoughts that inevitably arise: "One should just try to see the transitory nature, the translucent nature of thoughts. One should not become involved in them, nor reject them, but simply observe them and then come back to the awareness of breathing. The whole point is to cultivate the acceptance of everything so one should not discriminate or become involved in any kind of struggle."

By accepting everything, anticipating nothing, and letting all be as it will, you follow the instant-by-instant flow of your breath. Beneath the waves on the surface of the sea the water remains massively calm. Be like that calm. Become that calm.

"*Uncle, how can words that have no meaning even for the person who utters them be of any use at all, let alone assist his spiritual progress? . . . "*
Groping for a way of expressing this thought in English, he replied earnestly: "Words with meanings just good for ordinary use—not much power and get in your way like rocks upsetting a boat. Words with much power not show out real meaning—best forget meaning and keep mind free."

John Blofeld
Mantras, Sacred Words of Power

Attention to breathing has for centuries been the favorite device for focusing attention during meditation practice. However, the use of mantras also has a long history and has gained popularity in America and elsewhere thanks to the spread of Transcendental Meditation, which employs this device as the centerpiece of its method. The word mantra is Sanskrit and means prayer or hymn. A mantra is a short collection of sacred words. By continuous, silent repetition of a mantra one excludes all other thoughts from the mind. Initiates of Transcendental Meditation receive in secret a mantra of Sanskrit syllables that have no literal meaning. The meaninglessness of the mantra is in keeping with ancient tradition. Some say that the power of a Sanskrit formula resides within the sounds themselves and the physical vibrations they set off in the body of the practitioner. Whether or not there is any truth in this mystical view, I have found that the mental repetition of any short phrase can be an effective device for focusing attention.

The phrase need not be bestowed on you, nor be meaningless or foreign. A good mantra-like device could be the words, "I am one with all," for example. John Blofeld, a respected Chinese scholar who has made a study of mantras, thinks that the Jesus Prayer qualifies as a mantra. Its meaning, like the meaning of the phrase I suggest above, blurs and fades with constant repetition so that one's attention is not nagged by the verbal concept it signifies. It runs, "Lord Jesus Christ, Son of God, have mercy on us." If you find yourself particularly disturbed about one thing or another, so riled emotionally that you cannot calm yourself by attention to breath, try using a mantra in your meditation practice. I cannot recommend that you use the mantra exclusively, however, for there are problems with the mantra, the most difficult being to shed the mantra once a meditative habit becomes effective.

Another device for achieving an inward focus, and one that I personally find more helpful, is visualization. The Tibetans have used this device successfully for centuries. Simple or elaborate, the rewards are endless. Like the mantra, however, I feel that visualization should be investigated only after one has firmly established a meditation habit. In beginning visualization, or in using it to consolidate a meditation habit, it is wise to keep it simple. Use only two or three symbols: the circle, the square, or the triangle. In using any one of the three, close your eyes and let your mind see only the symbol. Do not study it. Do not expand or detail it. Use it to pass through.

Colors and music are excellent visualizations. Close your eyes and visualize a soft and benevolent blue mist. Breathe in the mist. Let its purity soothe and calm you. Or you may visualize yourself in a faraway golden green meadow. If you listen carefully, the geometry of musical sounds can be visualized. In the visualization, seat yourself comfortably for meditation. In this peaceful place nothing can disturb you. Allow its stillness to flow through you.

Strict disciplines or elaborate forms of creative meditation should only be considered after you have become established in the habits of exercise, diet, and basic meditation—after you have learned to do something *for* the self before doing anything *with* the self. Creative meditations are a development that, I believe, should only be entered into after one has had considerable practice in centering within and removing the self from the everyday, every-hour pressures of ordinary existence. The following method might be tried when you feel your meditative habit established in this way.

STATIONARY TRAVEL

Sit relaxed, preferably in a quiet room.
Spine erect.
Breathe slowly and deeply.
Begin to feel that you are completely relaxed, are letting go of the worries and excitement that grip your life.
Visualize a tiny dot of golden light in the middle of your forehead between your eyes.
Focus all your attention on that dot, that point between the eyes. Concentrate. At first it is a tiny dot, a spot that is hardly visible. Keep concentrating on it and, as you do, breathe deeply. When your attention is completely focused on the light you will no longer be aware of your breathing and be able to allow the spot to swell, begin to whiten, and shine brilliantly.
Just be a witness. Do not try to control the moment, do not make the spot glow. Soon it will begin to fill your forehead as you lose your self and feel and see that you are—you are the light. It is the presence of spirit that shines in every cell and every breath.

You will feel marvelously energized after such meditation. Seeing the light, bathing in light, connects you with inner energies that empower your total being. You can use this meditation to open channels blocked by stress or the anxiety of everyday problems, the true causes behind much illness. By visualizing light energies flowing smoothly throughout your body you harmoniously unify your whole being. In this respect meditation is a tool for healing not only your body and mind but your spirit as well, for it brings to awareness the positive essence that pervades each of us.

IV.

The initial contact with essence, with one's spiritual self, is one of complete elation. It is unutterably wonderful to discover and rediscover your full-dimensional self. Your newly expanded consciousness now includes a part of you that had been estranged. It is as if some final door of the neglected mansion has been opened and you have experienced the wonder beyond. Now you know the other realities and patterns of understanding that have been repeatedly promised.

You become available to energy and hope, which allows you to live a more meaningful life than you dared to imagine. That life you have been living, those dreary cycles of doubt, fear, and loneliness, will begin to evaporate like shallow dreams in the brilliant light of expanding consciousness. The archaic bondage you have become accustomed to has ended.

This elation, this intoxication, will gradually subside to be replaced by an ongoing sense of profound fulfillment. The onerous problems, as well as the grave challenges of daily life, still confront you but you are changed now and you meet them differently. You have slain the dragons of pettiness, pointlessness, and despair. Win, lose, or draw in the arena of daily affairs, your center is solid and immovable. *You know who you are.* As the sages say: You are in the world but not entirely of it. You are of a piece with the cosmos.

Meditation makes us aware of how the life we have been living limits, indeed separates us from the very concept of consciousness. It makes us aware of the impermanence of all that arises and passes. In our desires, in grasping for gratification, we have strayed far from love and loving. Like ignorant children we have indulged in inane pursuits that have kept us plying circular routes of gain and pain. We have gone out instead of going in, and by doing so have drifted from our centers and denied the existence of the wondrous living presence within.

Meditation shows that all this might have been necessary. As you must travel away from home to discover how precious home is, so it seems somehow necessary to live a conditioned experience in order to yearn for the unconditioned and limitless estate to which you were born. That is why you must be *ready* for meditation. For not until you feel the need to know yourself, to center, to gather in your energies, will meditation be undertaken with resolve and determination. Once resolved, however, nothing can stop you. Be who you are wherever you are. There is no need for a sect, an ashram, or a cave in a mountainside. Your ground is the ordinary, everyday world of the twentieth century, but you have a powerful refuge. Your unified body-mind-spirit is the vehicle of transcendence.

Do not be misled into believing there is something very solemn about this practice of meditation. Nothing could be more natural to who you really are, where you truly live.

Meditation is nothing but coming back home, just to have a little rest inside. It is not the chanting of a mantra, it is not even a prayer; it is just coming back home and having a little rest. Not going anywhere is meditation, just being where you are; there is no other "where"—just being there where you are, just occupying only that space where you are.

Bhagwan Shree Rajneesh
Only One Sky

The journey is not easy. Meditation, the key, is a difficult path and the way requires great patience and perseverance. It commands discipline, learning, and certain changes in your life before it will bring transformation you could not have planned for, could not even have imagined. Remember that the disciplines you practice through exercise and diet begin the transformation. As they conserve your body, meditation restores your spirit. The choice is yours. You alone can elect to stay unconscious, asleep, and unaware of human potential. Or you can seize the means of change.

5.

Lifestyle

*If it strikes the reader as presumptuous to
equate his personal center with the center of the cosmos, he must
be reminded that physics requires him to do just that; because
space is relative and curved, the center of the physical universe is
for each observer the point from which his observations proceed.*

Huston Smith
Forgotten Truth

I.

"Lifestyle" refers to the tangible and intangible modes which encompass our whole life. Included are attitudes, values, and priorities we hold as well as the environment in which we live and work and its material and psychological features. Lifestyle both expresses and determines individuality. Much of it is inherited or fixed and subject to little alteration, but certain crucial elements can be changed to agree with our desire to expand consciousness and participate in living awareness.

A lifestyle reflects a person's family background, the ethnic and regional inputs during the formative years of childhood, and the religious, educational, and socio-economic conditions that shaped that individual. Later determinants include the person's geographical location and particular community, occupation, and intimate relationships, as well as all of the rooms or houses the person has inhabited. Further elaborations are created by choices of home furnishings, clothes, transportation, the uses of leisure time, as well as the particular people and social activities

113

she or he prefers. It is these latter categories and elaborations that may be altered and improved, provided the person has the courage to thoughtfully examine the attitudes and values that sustain them. As always, the changes that matter proceed from the center within. "Give me a place to stand on," said an ancient Greek thinker, "and I will move the earth."

It's quite possible to follow a certain lifestyle and yet be unaware of all that it represents. Playing the self false, such people easily come to identify with various personas their certain lifestyles automatically provide. They become so attached to family, institutions, career, possessions, or ambitions that they forget their true identity: the mind-body-spirit self that alone imparts meaning to relationships or activities. To cling to the trappings of an imposed lifestyle and ignore its inner essence induces frustration and dissatisfaction. The multitudinous involvements in careers, families, friends, associates, communities, entertainments, politics, and religion confer an inhibiting and repetitious cycle that conflicts with true awareness and, indeed, leads away from inner peace and harmony. Those who get caught in endless demands of duty and rounds of questionable activity are usually afraid to miss out, to be left out or rejected, above all to be alone. Involvement becomes a stupefying alternative to awareness and change.

Even those who have begun to develop awareness often find it difficult to recognize activities and involvements that have become habitual or dictatorial. The questions of what to do and how to do what is needed can be endless and are best taken up one by one as they arise. I do not believe there can be any master plan for awareness or change, but my own experience is that a patient, systematic approach is essential. My approach is to examine and critically evaluate in turn the person, the home, the workplace, and society. Bear in mind that developing awareness and altering your lifestyle will eventually conflict with many material advantages and traditional attachments. By creating disciplines for exercise, diet, and meditation you have already begun to explore and benefit from the value of nonattachment, to be more self-contained. You will soon see the virtue of dropping negative relationships and discarding needless possessions. As you disengage and simplify your life you gain the confidence of knowing that you can live without the hindering habits and fixed ideas to which you were once attached and by which you were often ensnared. Once this process of change has begun it is inexorable and will affect you and everyone and everything around you. Recognizing this and preparing for what is bound to happen is of paramount importance! It is essential to be alert and responsible at all times, and to strictly avoid confusing or disorienting loved ones or close associates. Awareness must be unified in such a way that the ensuing changes in your lifestyle are a victory and a blessing for the whole network of your relationships, even those in which you no longer partake.

Never suffer an exception to occur till the new habit is securely rooted in your life. Each lapse is like the letting fall of a ball of string which one is carefully winding up; a single slip undoes more than a great many turns will wind again.

William James

We begin with the person. Begin by keeping a journal which will greatly increase awareness of your activities and motives. Lengthy self-examination is not necessary; in fact, it is undesirable. Just make brief notes at the end of every other day about what you did and why. Try to account for mornings, afternoons, evenings, not in detail but in general. Every so often, read back over the past week or two and make a critical appraisal of how you are using your energy and examine where the time has gone.

In my own case, I was continually shocked at the hours wasted in shopping and needless errands: precious time spent seeking or introducing into my life things I really did not need. I was upset at the extent to which shopping exposed me to the infection of advertising and the glare of material temptation. Not until I came to regard advertising as audio-visual pollution could I begin to escape its poisonous effect, for I was often snared by the glitter of its cartoonish qualities, by the colorized electricity of its clever distortion. Eventually, painfully, I learned to modify my response to this pollution, moving from not being bothered by it to feeling extremely insulted that it was forced upon me with such rude frequency and bad taste. While driving with the radio silenced I came to notice more of neighborhood and countryside. At home, I indulged my love of music with a greater investment in records and tapes, and I drastically reduced time in front of the television by making careful program selections. By conducting ordered evaluations of mail order catalogs and print advertisements, I was able to fill my needs as they arose, solving most of my shopping problems. There was no question of deprivation or missing out as advertisers would have me believe, but a simple matter of carefully defining needs and, above all, protecting that privacy that an awareness of consciousness requires.

A journal can help you learn to use energy more wisely and conserve privacy, but it requires honestly confronting your motives and questioning your use of time. For example, how much of what you do is to escape loneliness or avoid difficult confrontation with the self? How often are you killing time in order to evade the demands of change? Although such self-examination may be painful, the rewards for purging materialistic anti-life attitudes are considerable. In doing this remember to be fair and kind with yourself, not harsh. Try not to condemn or be judgmental. Instead, just notice and evaluate how each day is lived. Then decide, in the light of a long-range goal to expand awareness, what must be changed. A journal can also serve as a tool for healing and letting go of emotional wounds and pain caused by past incidents or events you were unable to face or previously understand. Exercising forgiveness through understanding those who may have harmed you—intentionally or unintentionally—is a powerful way toward freeing energy and further expanding awareness.

Another example from my own personal experience—as I learned to use time more productively and to cherish privacy—was that I saw less of those people in my life who through confusion and misunderstanding occasionally mocked my interest in health and awareness. Harmful gossip, jaded or fatalistic remarks about finances or politics, negative statements about the workplace, morbid comments about the state of friends, introduced bad opera I did not need. Talk about acquisitions, recent sexual detente and sensational vogue pushed me toward real and imagined arenas of snarling competition from which I was determined to escape. Withdrawal from such relationships produced no regrets on either side, yet for those who wondered or sincerely inquired, I was available and glad to share my interests within the bounds I was gradually establishing for myself.

With honesty you acknowledge certain activities you may still indulge in that are not only habitual but physically detrimental. Alcohol, nicotine, and caffeine, though legal and socially acceptable, are lethal in the danger they pose and the havoc they wreak in exchange for illusionary rewards—relief when you are depressed and relaxation when you are satisfied. But when indulged, these habits extract an intolerably high toll. Excessive alcohol not only destroys lives, it drains and too often ruinously squanders human energy, and in America creates more economic devastation than any other substance. A cigarette not only tastes and smells bad, but is dangerous to the health of the non-smoker. As for caffeine, some recent studies claim that caffeine may have potentially harmful effects.

Everyone knows these substances are both expensive and completely nonessential to existence. Yet people persist because they have made a choice to remain attached to the habit or because they are addicted to the effects—the highs. *The key is that a similar choice of nonattachment can be made.* Habit is a product of accepted activity. To counteract this acceptance the visualization of an unbiased witness within the self is needed to provide a fresh perspective and enable a new awareness to emerge. One stands aside, like a witness, watches the repetitive reach, examines the desire for an additional cup of coffee, a smoke, or a drink. One sees how boredom, loneliness, or social pressure promotes needless actions. In every likelihood it can be seen that a subtle addiction has taken hold, a network of need has tightened. This awareness may be silly or shocking, but allow it to galvanize you into recognizing the source of these actions and ultimately eliminate them from your repertoire. Only through a new awareness of the activity can the negative effects be seen with broad enough detachment, and only then can appropriate change be initiated.

This same detachment is needed to appraise the material excess in your life. As you acquire habits and styles more in tune with your determination to develop awareness and utilize consciousness, you will become skilled at consulting the witness and directing attention to the accumulation of furnishings and miscellaneous possessions that occupy your spaces. You will better see and decide what is truly useful to the new realities and actions you are cultivating. You will be free to get rid of what is not useful. Clutter of any kind hinders your progress. You can live a larger life by eliminating countless "things" once considered necessary, "things" that are the legacy of an infectious materialism that subverts how you live. Call on the witness often and heed the counsel of detachment. Making reassessment your guiding principle will create an increasingly open environment in which both deep meaning and light-filled enchantment enter each day.

I shall only look up and say, "Who am I then?" Tell me that first, and then if I like being that person, I'll come up; if not, I'll stay down here till I'm somebody else.
Lewis Carroll
Alice in Wonderland

II.

Expanded consciousness on any level, practical or otherwise, dissolves much of the familiar and leads beyond the known. Precisely because the newly emerging synthesis is full of promise, it is likely some confusion and uncertainty will be experienced in this process of transformation and transcendence. The fabulous potential of expanded consciousness can be dazzling in an alluring rainbow of possibility that includes the new paradigms found in physics, biofeedback, holistic healing, parapsychology, Eastern and Western religions, tarot, astrology, and the rich assortment of occult methods. At the same time, you may feel an ambivalence about the dissolution of external authority you have effected. Obviously, every possibility offered need not be explored or even seriously considered. So how shall you decide which explorations, if any, to undertake?

There is no reason to be intimidated by any of the possibilities of consciousness, but there is every reason to be contained within yourself before exploring any of them, certainly before exposing yourself to new authority. And there is every reason to remember that centering must be based on a lifestyle of which you are the ultimate architect and judge. Uncertainty, doubt, or confusion can be resolved after consideration and meditation and through a balanced trust in how you feel about the question at hand, whether it be a matter of attending a seminar on reincarnation, healing, or past lives; participating in a Gestalt workshop; or delving further into some event of religious significance. *To establish and maintain your center is crucial.* In particular, experimenting with drugs should never be encouraged or attempted before this is accomplished. I am speaking of drugs used to alter consciousness, which begin with sugar, nicotine, caffeine, and alcohol and climb a scale past marijuana and hashish, up toward mescaline, peyote, and LSD.

Although I avoid drugs, I realize that for centuries people from many cultures and religions have used drugs as agents, devices, or helpers in order to explore and go beyond ordinary awareness. Peyote and mescaline are part of the religious ceremonies of certain American Indian groups. In India, ganja is used by some yogis and spiritual people. In his highly regarded 1972 book, *The Natural Mind*, Andrew Weil points out the fundamental fascination with altered states of consciousness, "We seem to be born with a drive to experience episodes of altered consciousness. This drive expresses itself at very early ages in all children in activities designed to cause loss or major disturbance of ordinary awareness." In the United States, the use of drugs and the experience of altered states have been little understood and, for the most part, badly practiced. Also, of course, such usage is illegal, although the prohibition has probably done as much to spur as to deter experimentation. The complete comprehension of altered states of consciousness is still well beyond us and has hardly been clarified by scientific or creative investigation. For those who may wish to seriously use drugs or psychedelic agents, despite the illegality, there are a few simple rules based on common sense:

1. In using any agent have respect for its properties. Do not allow it to overwhelm you. Keep dosage below a base minimum.

2. Alcohol should never be used as a consciousness-altering substance, especially with other agents.

3. The most common agents, marijuana and hashish, are usually smoked, but smoking anything for any purpose is not conducive to health and awareness. Marijuana and hashish are best prepared in tea.

4. Mescaline and peyote should never be used without an experienced guide with whom spiritual rapport has been established.

5. When seeking an altered state through an agent it is imperative to know what you are using and prepare for the experience through several days of meditation and fasting.

6. Practical preparation—the when and where—should be considered along with deep respect for effects.

Sound information on drugs and altered states is limited by the fact that tolerance for both is always subjective. Objectivity is inevitably lost in the confusion brought about by political and religious institutions, and public opinion has been prejudiced against any experiment with altered states of consciousness. Therefore it is advisable that considerable time be spent in critical review of the wisdom of any drug use. The key is caution. No matter what your background or previous experience, it is best to broaden awareness through the implementation of an exercise program, a lifetime diet, a habit of meditation, and a firmly centered, chosen lifestyle before experimenting with altered states, whether induced by drugs or religious experience.

What needs to be remembered is that agents or devices are not necessary. The New Age has revealed much evidence that highs induced by external means have little to do with raising consciousness. The efforts of Stanislav Grof have confirmed this. Since 1985, Grof, a respected psychiatrist and one of the pioneers in LSD research, has been proving that altered states can be reached without drugs. Holotropic Therapy, or what has become known as "the Grof work," focuses on breathing—as well as music, movement, and art work—as a means of loosening psychological defenses and releasing unconscious material. Many spiritual authorities claim that no agent or device exceeds the power of meditation. Speaking on the use of drugs, the yogi Swami Muktananda has pointed out, "Meditation affects extremely refined sensory nerves for which drugs . . . are much too strong. Those nerves cannot even bear strong coffee. Furthermore, meditation is more intoxicating than drugs could ever be . . . far more potent than ganja." Any advantage agents might have would have to be measured against the potential effects that "tripping" might have on the routines of normal existence.

The final rule about consciousness-altering agents is as follows: *No experience should be sought which would disrupt the daily care of your body and mind, your relationships, or your livelihood.*

III.

A carefully considered journal can do more than record your use of time and help reevaluate relationships. It can preserve your concern with the inner aspects of your lifestyle, particularly the all-but-unconscious habits and long-held attachments that affect your beginning efforts and sensibilities. Again, heightened awareness arising from your center is the basis of meaningful alterations of lifestyle. And these, in turn, will inform the changes deemed useful in the outer aspects of your person. The following are some examples which may be considered.

Make a regular survey of the surface of your body. Be aware of any irritated reactions of the skin and scalp that may be caused by allergies. These signals of discomfort should be taken as a sign that what you are eating or using on your body may be wrong for, or harmful to, your system. They can also be signs of stress. Integrating sound nutrition with daily exercise, an occasional fast, and meditation is the very best long-term way to take care of your skin and hair. The use of natural products and hot baths for this purpose is also recommended. Of course, any serious signs should be brought to the attention of your physician.

In regard to make-up, I believe women should stay away from most commercial cosmetics as much as possible. Whenever possible, use skin cleansers, lotions and deodorants that are not perfumed and are generally hypo-allergenic. In the 1990s, fortunately, there are countless natural items that are good for hair and skin. For example, aloe vera gel heals all kinds of irritations. The pure extract of the aloe vera plant is usually inexpensive and can be purchased in any well-stocked health-food store. However, no matter what external care is provided, it should be remembered that the wholesome foods we eat not only provide nutrition but also can be used in skin and hair care. There are many natural alternatives to commercial cosmetics.

These are but a few alternatives. Local bookstores, libraries or health-food stores all offer marvelous material on the subject that you can consult for other suggestions.

Make-up is an advantage as well as a burden we women have carried for centuries. Advertisements continually attempt to condition us into believing that we cannot get along without it. Part of the problem is a denial of aging. Americans

SIMPLE ATTENTION

Splash water on your face. Make a lather with a handful of finely ground almonds or oats and smooth onto your face. Rinse with water and pat dry.

You can experiment with a variety of fresh or dried herbs, such as mint and parsley, as facial cleansers. Sage makes an excellent astringent wash. Herbs are also good for the hair as a natural rinse. Try rubbing a slice of raw potato or cucumber on your face before washing, or make a face mask out of mashed avocados, which are also good for the hair as a conditioner. Mayonnaise massaged into the hair and left in place an hour before shampooing makes a great conditioner as well.

Pure almond or apricot oil is excellent as a skin emollient and can be used on both face and body.

worship the bloom of youth and attempt to fight back and hide the physical changes that maturation brings. However, for any woman to deny her experience of time is to stunt her own growth. Still, the dream of youth persists and, since no elixir exists, we cling to the promise of make-up. That we should ever find ourselves without make-up! The attachment is formidable but not insurmountable. Make-up, after all, is only one of many ways to enhance appearance. Being cognizant of alternatives is another. It is easier to remember that true attractiveness, true beauty, reflects from within. The whole person can become enhanced by changes brought on through the physical advantages of inner energy. Make-up, at best, becomes a superfluous luxury and its use should be modulated as inner magnetism increases.

Next to meditation, baths are always a prime source of relaxation, especially after work. Men, who rarely use the bath properly, seldom realize that the psychological benefits of a bath are quite different from those of a shower. The running water of a shower is best for cleansing the body. Once cleansed, soaking in a hot bath is incomparably relaxing, particularly if ceremony is created through burning incense, dimming lights and using a small amount of oil to melt tension as well as ego. Retreats to the sauna or steam bath are even better.

In the United States and Europe we are pressured by changing fashion to spend beyond our means for clothing. Not only are good clothes expensive but they usually require special care, which can be a continual expense. Dress is central to an expression of personality, yet we seldom think about why we dress as we do. Clothing both protects and adorns the body, but it should also provide personal aesthetic pleasure before any professional or social statement of who we are. In no case should it be allowed to become a conduit into inescapable credit balances. A wardrobe can be an attachment wherein there never seems to be enough of the right sort of shoes, suits, shirts, coats, hats, or whatever desires have been created by advertising that literally causes us to wear our debts.

The paramount benefit of a revised lifestyle is to stop being victimized in this way. The more aware we become, the more we see the value in shedding attachments to countless things that, day after day and year after year, do nothing but clutter our lives and warp our finances.

Acting on awareness, make a systematic evaluation of yourself, your wardrobe, your home, and your transportation needs. Establish a plan in which you buy only what you need only when you need it. Avoid the traps of fashion, and determine your own style. Choose apparel made of natural fibers, such as cotton and wool. Although costlier than synthetic fabrics, natural fibers tend to be more durable and suitable for passing through the elusive internal changes with which you must contend. All the elements of dress should combine in a kind of neutral disguise in which you are perfectly at ease. Footwear is of the greatest importance. Insist on buying for the health and comfort of your feet, as you prepare to walk and wander more. Walking, especially in the woods, on the beach, or by a stream, is not only a wonderful exercise but an activity that frees us to see and appreciate more. Above all, it allows immediate contact with the earth that grounds us, and the air we breathe.

IV.

The home is the second major area of lifestyle. There is always a need to reassess where you live, how you live there, and why. Are you satisfied where you are? Is it comfortable and pleasing to you, or did you move into it for convenience or as an investment? The apartment or house you dwell in should serve more as a shelter and retreat than an investment. Make it the place, the refuge, that provides you with privacy, atmosphere, and removal from the rush of raw life. With organized effort anyone can find a place in which she or he may create a better shelter.

If you are married and/or live with children, the problems of living awareness are increased and will have to be openly discussed. Additional space might be required in order to afford more privacy. You may want to plan for more room to accommodate children or a relative who lives with you. This may mean moving. In all probability it might mean moving into a less expensive neighborhood, a suburb, or out to the countryside. In the climate of today's mercurial real estate market, it could mean moving back into the neglected heart of the city. Whatever the alternative, if you have a need or desire for more space or privacy, by all means do something about it. To give up a convenient or fashionable address for a larger, more practical dwelling in order to gain privacy and freedom from financial involvement can easily be misunderstood. However, you can spare yourself long explanations or justifications to friends and associates. In concert with your family and/or children, make the decisions and follow those decisions with appropriate moves. Just do it! In the long run, it will prove to be a sound and sensible step for those determined to escape the spiraling systems that engulf all of us.

I once lived on a houseboat in a quiet harbor tucked under two green foothills. I found solitude there and was able to get in tune with myself and nature. The ceaseless movement of the water and the calm circling of the white gulls added to the inner silence I gathered from my practice. This home provided a space of tranquility, a passageway to inner worlds. After fasting, after replenishing my energies, I was well-fortified to return to the world of travel and revolving traffic, and the strain that goes with work and foreign cities. Although I am married and share another home with my husband today, I still find time to retreat to the rhythms of a harbor or the sands of a shore. There I simply sit, gazing out across the water. The sounds put me in touch with a natural order of earth, sky, and sea, and ultimately a concern with my own fragile being.

To make decisions opting for greater awareness and change often seems simplistic and can be easily ridiculed. This can stem from a quality of fear that change creates. The varieties and circumstances are different for everyone. It may mean dealing with complex questions like where to live and what to do with a pet. If that pet is unruly and difficult to have around, you might have to make a decision to find another home for it or take it to an animal shelter. Many will think this an insensitive decision, but it is better than continuing with the irritation of not being able to adequately provide for the animal. Letting go of a bothersome pet does not mean you love animals less but that you have gained clear command of the limits of your inhabited spaces. You might get another pet, one more suited to your task and environment. Birds can be cheerful companions that require a minimum of care and allow loving, positive vibrations. Fish can also bring calm to your living space, and the enigmatic cat is always an ally of meditation.

Whatever you do, reevaluate all of your furnishings, the colors of your walls, your use of lighting and floor space, curtains and rugs. Think in terms of comfort and space rather than fashion or whatever material value anything might possess. Furniture, an important aspect of any lifestyle, can always be rearranged, but do not hesitate to get rid of a cumbersome piece that no longer serves a purpose. The colors in your home should soothe and aesthetically enhance the privacy of your environment. If necessary, repaint. It is relatively easy to do and can be an exercise in exerting control, not to mention the personal satisfaction of doing something to initiate change.

It is always important to reconsider lighting. Install dimmers if you do not already have them. Unless you are reading or doing other close work, direct electric light is hard on the eyes, wastes energy, and usually violates any atmosphere that you have tried to create. Dimmers allow you to control the level of light and adjust it to changing needs. Candles are excellent for softer lighting and, if scented, can add to the quality of the air as well. The use of stained glass adds delicate beauty to a window and wondrously alters the character of a room.

The most obvious addition to any living space is plants. Not only do they add color, they help establish a rapport between you and nature and bring you back to balanced aspects of your life. The right plants will thrive in any positive atmosphere. Flowers and plants are delightful, silent companions that add oxygen to the air in your rooms. Treat them as pets or special friends. Talk to them, play music for them, and let them know when you are leaving for a few days. You will profit from the magic such an exchange can produce.

When and wherever possible start a garden. Whether of flowers, vegetables, or both, a garden takes you outdoors and adds to your rapport with the earth. There is also a tremendous satisfaction in knowing that at least some of the food you eat and flowers that you enjoy are trusted products of your own hand and available right outside of your door. It is often amazing what a six-foot-square plot can produce. An interesting experiment is to compare a vegetable purchased at the store with the same kind grown in your own yard. Boil two pots of water. Place the store produce near one and go to your garden and pick its twin. Cook the two for equal amounts of time and serve separately. The difference is enlightening.

In earlier chapters I have spoken about two of the most important spaces in the home, the kitchen and the area used for meditating. I pointed out that the meditation area is best reserved exclusively for this activity. It is also advisable, whenever possible, to restrict other areas of the home to specific activities—the dining room for meals; the living room for social gatherings, conversation and listening to music; a study or library for reading, journal-writing, and keeping household accounts. A separate space for television viewing is a good idea, particularly if there are children or others in the household who watch regularly.

The omnipresent problem of attachment to objects and habits constantly needs to be reviewed and refined. It is one thing to become involved in discourse and contemplation about attachment—and quite another to reduce the lofty ideas and ideals down to a level where we begin to act and make a difference in our lives. The value of attachments can be elusive and painful as well as comic. Not only are we attached to objects or habits, but we can be attached by them.

Telephones are perhaps the best example. They have been wired into our lives as *the* means of communication. Yet convenient as they are, they are not always the best means of communication. As I noted in the beginning of this book, the handwritten note or letter has a quality other means of communication seldom equal. Even a postcard can impart meaning a phone call can never convey. Often the best business can be conducted more sensibly through the mail. Even as alternatives are used, however, the telephone is often connected in too many households and too many automobiles. It was ironic how, when I first began to practice meditation or wished to withdraw for a day of solitude, I could easily refrain from using the phone but could do little to escape its ring. Smothering the phone under pillows helped muffle the noise so that I could ignore it and hold myself still until the ringing ceased, but the privacy or meditative state was always ruptured by the intrusion. When I first thought about having the telephone put on a plug, I dismissed the idea as silly and extreme. Nevertheless, I overcame the hesitation and ordered the plug. The first time I unplugged the instrument to spend a day alone I could sense the difference of insured silence. It was a long weekend in which I had set aside time for relaxation and meditation and it proved unforgettable. Released, I used the time so profitably that I kept the telephone unplugged for what turned into an emotional vacation. I recovered my old journal and brought it up to date and, leaving to go to the grocery store I decided to leave my car at the curb and walk. After shopping I rode a bus back home. I had not used a bus in years. It took me back to my girlhood when the bus was my only means of transportation. The freedom from driving and parking felt luxurious! It liberated me from what had literally become a mechanical trap. In the years that followed I realized how that walk introduced me to the subsequent pleasures of walking in quiet districts, to the serenity of an hour or day of undisturbed silence, all but forgotten in the business of life. Unless we take direct action to avoid traps, we will be continuously bombarded by the clangor of machinery and by systems that electronically suck at the vulnerable surface of our attention.

After having the plug installed in the phone I experimented further by disconnecting the radio and television for a three-week period and reducing my newspaper subscription to the Sunday edition. At the time these simple moves were great fodder for the jokes of cynical friends, but they proved telling. I had somehow permitted myself to become enslaved by the technologies of the day. Worse, I was paying them to do it to me. These changes, small though they seemed then, helped deliver me from enthrallment. The quality of my privacy deepened and the territory of my home widened in a way I had not thought possible. I urge you to try these things for yourself. You may find as I did that, after all, there is nothing to lose but your chains.

V.

The key to creating the lifestyle you want is to recapture control of what you do and choose where you do it. It is the formation of a process through which a person begins to live those actions usually relegated to the edges of wishful thinking. In this section we will look at some of the major contact points between an individual lifestyle and the surrounding society and examine practical ways to transform wishes into reality.

The best place to begin is to train yourself out of credit. Credit is never an advantage to the user, especially in today's climate. Buy-now-pay-later has become the sly decoy of our tomorrows. Next week, next month, next year—how smoothly the system operates to get us to surrender our options for the future. It may take months or several years to face your economic reality and turn your life around in this respect, but if you are to develop an awareness of consciousness it must be done. As you generate discipline in performing exercises, in cultivating your lifetime diet, in learning to remove yourself through meditation, so there is a need to develop discipline in handling money. Money is a green energy of existence and unless you establish control over it, it will consume you. Make a determined effort by destroying credit cards. If you must have credit standing, limit the number of cards to no more than two, a gasoline card, say, and a travel card such as American Express or an all-purpose bank card. Whenever possible, pay with cash or use traveler's checks. Only by doing so will you better see and feel where your money goes. All it requires is that you spend more time on your personal budget. If nothing else this will provide an enlightening review of expenditures which, in turn, will disclose patterns of spending. These patterns can be analogous to those of time and energy. As the lifelong consumption of white sugar poisons the body, the use of credit paralyzes the potential freedom of any individual. With the same slow, treacherous infection the use of credit builds a never-ending network of compromise that subverts the possibility of change. Like the savings and loan bailout, personal credit has become a plague from which only an aware individual can escape.

Living within one's income is a lost art, a timeless social value that is also an important principle for all who strive to gain and remain in control of their lives. Another social value that can no longer be ignored is captured in the slogan, "A day's work for a day's pay." Some skeptics may make much of that, however our means of livelihood consumes a major portion of every day. Whatever our job may be, there is a need for a kind of zen intention in order to keep it from disrupting the tenor of our lifestyle. In modern America it might be possible that the corporation, profession, craft, or service within which we carry out our work may not deserve our best, but certainly our self-respect does. At the same time, however, our livelihood should be kept quite separate from our private life. The separation needs to be maintained in such a way that we enjoy a diversity of contacts with people from all walks of life, including those who are not working on the development of awareness. Some assessment of how much a job takes from private life has to be made. Are our employers being fair about recognizing our contribution? Are the services or products we produce necessary or worthwhile? Have the ethical and ecological ramifications been honestly considered? Today, more than ever, these are questions that cannot be overlooked.

Dedication to a job to the degree that it increases stress is the tragic basis of the materialistic snare. Recent research has shown that job promotion can induce stress, which may, in turn, increase the possibility of heart attack or cancer. This is but one reason why there is a continual need to devote attention to defining and preserving the meaning of life. In truth we are not living *for* a profession, a product, or corporation, or even for our family. And certainly not for the economic stability of our community or nation. We are living *with* them. It is not always easy to separate what we do from who we are or what we want to do, but we must remember that the problem of alienation is often a blessing. Nevertheless, balancing the demands of job involvement against time needed for inner development is vital, and must be honestly arranged. Without honest arrangement it is impossible to establish the balance whereby we maintain control of the quality of our activities.

A person who sets out to live consciously begins in an exploited world, one in which she or he is led to believe that nothing can be done. Science promised us the earth, but its technologies are dooming us with pesticides and pollutants. Political and business leaders continue to endorse and finance these technologies on a trial-and-error basis. In spite of the grave mistakes of the past most of these "authorities" believe in chemical medicine and nuclear power. Amid massive controversy over the side effects of medicines and the perils of nuclear waste—all-too-real catalysts for personal or wholesale catastrophe—individual awareness can be whirled away or subverted for the sake of "progress." But the subversion can no longer be excused. The pollution of our air and water and the criminal cutting of forests are so wrong that we must speak out. We must explore the power of awareness. Only then can we find meaning in our own world. Carl Jung wrote:

. . . war has thrown out the unanswerable accusation to civilized man that he is still a barbarian, and at the same time it has shown what inflexible retribution lies in store for him whenever he is tempted to make his neighbor responsible for his own bad qualities. Yet the psychology of the individual corresponds to the psychology of the nations. Only in the change of attitude of the individual can begin the change in the psychology of the nation.

The discovery of personal purpose renews faith that we can effect needed reforms and uphold the ethics of humanism in our world.

The rise of consciousness is still viewed with alarm by some social critics. As far back as 1976, it was argued that the interest in consciousness had serious social consequences. In *The New York Review of Books*, Christopher Lasch wrote:

The retreat to purely personal satisfactions—such as they are—is one of the main themes of the seventies. A growing despair of changing society—even of understanding it—has generated . . . a cult of expanded consciousness, health and personal growth . . . Having no hope of improving their lives in the ways that matter, people have convinced themselves that what matters is psychic self-improvement: getting in touch with their feelings, eating health foods . . . jogging . . . learning how to "relate" . . . To live for the moment is the prevailing passion—to live for yourself, not for your predecessors or posterity. We are fast losing the sense of historical continuity . . .

I feel such an attitude fails to acknowledge the degree to which current conventional lifestyle destroys our health and our spirit. It denatures us. How can we improve our lives "in ways that matter" when the cost of medical and health care has soared beyond the financial capability of many Americans? When lack of proper diet and nutrition has produced problems of epidemic levels; when stress has helped create an increase in cancer and heart disease; and when political ineptitude and inflation stalks the domesticity of everyone? The common activity of daily life has become so electrified that even to remember predecessors or find a moment in which to contemplate posterity has become a luxury. Our psychic, social, and political conditions have gone berserk, and every well-meaning attempt to restore decency and sanity to our collective life is chewed in the maws of that madness, co-opted and perverted to the uses of material development.

I feel there is only one choice the thinking individual can make: go within. Go within and patiently rediscover the self. Go within and begin the change, initiate a spiritual healing process. Without this return, the concerned individual melts into the computerized mass, the driven multitudes who are lost or unaware of the emergency. In beginning spiritual exploration you step beyond this level.

Responding to the doubts and feelings of your inner and outer being you instinctively change your condition by assuming responsibility for who you are and how you live. This action determines your future which, in turn, sets the tone of all communal life.

UNIFICATION

Unified awareness offers an alternative to the person who is a "stranger and afraid" in a world she or he never made. It offers a natural spirituality that transcends the religiosity of ego. Natural spirituality can define your life and enable you to master the material world you live in, a world in which you seek a way to grow. This is where you learn to live dual lives—one in the conditioned reality of the material world and the other as a free spirit of the cosmos. By unifying awareness you may hope to achieve your birthright as a child of God. Too many religious and psychospiritual systems call for various forms of surrender that are an integral part of their methods. These systems should be entered into—if you so choose—only after your own unification, not as a consequence of highly impressive exposures to powerful persons, sources, or forms. The way of such surrender is real but it is a subtle path for which "many are called but few are chosen."

Thus, expanded consciousness grows from self-responsibility, discipline, and careful, holistic practice. We know it does little good just to jog or eat a sound diet. By itself meditation may become a foil to the ego. Without a unified approach we are ever susceptible to disorientation in which time, direction, and energy are lost in confused shortcuts. There are no shortcuts really; only patient, continuous practice produces the necessary awareness.

Meditation is an excellent means to explore the human drama, to understand why we live, and continue to live even in death. It reveals that the mind contains everything. It clearly shows us how we are usually limited to a local awareness, a tiny patch of the vast domain of consciousness. How the revelation of all that ever has been, is, and will be, is blocked from the start because of our refusal to utilize the power of aging and explore the mystery of death. In an age in which we can launch space colonies is it too much to hope that our society will drop its taboos on death, easing the way for a concerned individual to reclaim death as part of the human experience? On levels of ordinary awareness, we continue to fear death and refuse to explore its nature or prepare for its coming. How we choose to live should determine the quality of our death as well as that of our life. When we allow ourselves to be limited by the common politics of science, religion, and traditional authority, we fail to honor our calling as perceptive beings.

Tread carefully. Do not forget where the final responsibility lies. Always be discriminating about where you put your trust. The most trustworthy of all, as you will inevitably discover, is your intuitive inner essence that is your true guide.

The pursuit may be lonely at times, especially in the beginning. Some people will not be as understanding as you wish. They may even feel angry or sarcastic, thinking that your attitudes implicitly condemn them or their way of life. This is not so, cannot be so, for this path of awareness is founded on kindness and compassion. Be alert to the feelings of others as you attend to yourself. From time to time you may find yourself exposed to and threatened by strong criticism and hostile vibrations of others. Should you be in situations with people who cause or project negativity, remain calm and generate positive energy to protect your own atmosphere. To keep such negative vibrations from penetrating and disrupting your peace, visualize lines of separation between your space and those who may misunderstand you. They instinctively realize that through a unified control of exercise, diet, and meditation, not only have your feelings changed but your thinking has changed as well. As much as you may wish to share this practice, whatever you do, do not try to change anyone. Allow others to discover for themselves the need for other awareness. In this way you will eventually be a truer friend to all around you.

Perhaps because my job called on me to continually attend to the needs and desires of others, I particularly treasured solitude. A time for solitude may be rare, but when allowed it brings infinite rewards, even those surprises and moments of inner stormy climes that may trigger the most profound insights. I believe we all need to experience solitude. Periods in which we organize quiet removal in order to establish inner balance and become truly centered. In the beginning, the practice of living awareness is an uphill struggle. There is so much ruckus and rowdiness in the world and so much chatterboxing constantly in one's own head. We need this solitude and silence at frequent intervals and when we achieve it the stillness becomes spacious, and in that infinite space we allow all and everything simply to be. Then all things reveal qualities we previously have missed or, worse, ignored. All of a sudden we may, if we persevere, perceive that we are not separate from, but part of, all that surrounds us. The perception flees the very instant it is recognized.

When alone, I am not lonely. There are never enough hours for the walks I want to take, the books I would like to read. In my journal I learned to purge layers of plastic personality, fears locked inside. Those efforts attracted me to Zen, and as I investigated the teachings of Zen Buddhism I came to see that the life I was living was the life I had always lived, and that it was not going to be substantially changed by death. All that I had done, all that I was doing, and all that I would do was a process of growth, toward an expansion of consciousness that was boundless. Through Zen meditation I discovered that my present was my past and future, and they formed a concurrent existence that took me beyond previous borders. I was capable of endless recognitions. It brought a harmony, a new meaning of peace and freedom when I realized that the veil of illusion under which I had once lived covered the simple tools of awareness.

Each of us contains a boundless well of energy that remains untapped within the "hara," the center of our being. Utilizing that energy, changing the style of one's life, requires time and careful consideration, flexible yet persistent effort. Rigidity hinders growth and impedes the recognition of the self as a whole being alive with energy, light, and love, vibrant with creativity and untold potential. The practice of awareness avoids extremes. The true challenge lies within you and your awareness of who you are and where you are at any and every given moment. Always *at* and *in* the present.

The key is to flow with this awareness that expands your consciousness, trusting your inner voice. To learn a loving kindness and forgiveness not only toward others but to yourself. Rest assured that the negative past becomes positive food for development as you grow from new experience. You have evolved and will keep evolving. The essential is intangible and to perceive the intangible is the blessed grace of equanimity. To live in harmony with both the material and spiritual aspects of your life requires courage, compassion, and patience. The courage to be different, to dissolve the attachments of materialism. The compassion for other people, other forms of life, and for all things. And the patience that arises from trusting in this path of wonder and change.

Bibliography

Ballentine, Rudolph. *Diet and Nutrition: A Holistic Approach*. Honesdale, Pa: Himalayan International Institute, 1978.

Bateson, Gregory. *Steps to an Ecology of Mind*. New York: Ballantine Books, 1972.

Blofeld, John. *Mantras: Sacred Words of Power*. New York: E.P. Dutton, 1977.

Borysenko, Joan. *Minding the Body, Mending the Mind*. New York: Simon & Shuster, 1988.

Boyd, Doug. *Rolling Thunder*. New York: Dell Publishing, 1977.

Briggs, Robert. *The American Emergency: A Search for Spiritual Renewal in an Age of Materialism*. Berkeley, Ca.: Celestial Arts, 1989.

Brown, Edward Espie. *The Tassajara Recipe Book*. Boston, Ma.: Shambhala Publications, Inc., 1985.

Bucke, R.M. *Cosmic Consciousness*. New York: E.P. Dutton, 1960.

Buksbazen, John Daishin. *To Forget the Self*. Los Angeles, Ca.: Zen Center of Los Angeles, 1977.

Campbell, Joseph. *Hero with a Thousand Faces*. New York: World Publishing Co. Reprint: Meridian Book Edition, 1956.

Campbell, Joseph. *The Masks of God: Creative Mythology*. New York: Viking Press, 1968.

Cannon, Walter B. *The Wisdom of the Body*. New York: W.W. Norton, 1942.

Capra, Frijof. *The Tao of Physics*. Berkeley, Ca.: Shambhala Publications, Inc., 1975.

Casteneda, Carlos. *The Teachings of Don Juan*. New York: Simon & Shuster, 1968.

Cox, Harvey. *Turning East*. New York: Simon & Shuster, 1977.

de Chardin, P. Teilhard. *The Phenomenon of Man*. Translated by B. Wall. New York: Harper Torchbooks, 1961.

de Ropp, Robert S. *Drugs and the Mind*. New York: Delacorte Press, 1957.

de Ropp, Robert S. *The Master Game*. New York: Delacorte Press, 1968.

de Ropp, Robert S. *Warrior's Way*. New York: Delacorte Press, 1979.

Dubos, Rene. *So Human an Animal*. New York: Charles Scribner's Sons, 1968.

Dufty, William. *Sugar Blues*. Radnor, Pa.: Chilton, 1975.

Durkheim, Karlfried G. *Hara: The Vital Center of Man*. London: Unwin Paperbacks, 1977.

Ewald, Ellen Buchman. *Recipes for a Small Planet*. New York: Ballantine Books, 1973.

Feldenkrais, Moshe. *Awareness through Movement*. New York: Harper & Row, 1972.

Feuerstein, George. *Encyclopedic Dictionary of Yoga*. New York: Paragon House, 1990.

Goldstein, Joseph and Jack Kornfield. *Seeking the Heart of Wisdom*. Boston, Ma.: Shambhala Publications, Inc., 1987.

Goleman, Daniel. *The Varieties of the Meditative Experience*. New York: E.P. Dutton, 1977.

Grof, Stan and Christina, *Spiritual Emergency*. Los Angeles, Ca.: J.P. Tarcher, 1989.

Gurdjieff, G.I. *Meetings with Remarkable Men*. New York: E.P. Dutton, 1963.

Haich, Elizabeth. *Initiation*. Palo Alto, Ca: Seed Center, 1960.

Huxley, Aldous. *The Doors of Perception*. New York: Harper & Row, 1954.

Iyengar, B.K.S. *Light on Yoga*. New York: Schocken, 1987.

Jung, C.J. *Psychological Reflections*. New York: Harper & Row, 1953.

Kapleau, P. *Three Pillars of Zen*. Boston: Beacon Press, 1967.

Kapleau, Phillip, ed. *The Wheel of Death: A Collection of Writings from Zen Buddhist and Other Sources on Death-Rebirth-Dying*. New York: Harper & Row, 1971.

Katzen, Mollie. *Still Life with Menu Cookbook*. Berkeley, Ca.: Ten Speed Press, 1988.

Keen, Sam. *Voices and Visions*. New York: Harper & Row, 1970.

Keleman, Stanley. *Living Your Dying*. New York: Random House/Bookworks, 1974.

Keleman, Stanley. *Your Body Speaks Its Mind*. New York: Simon & Shuster, 1975.

Keleman, Stanley. *Emotional Anatomy*. Berkeley, Ca.: Center Press, 1985.

Krishna, Gopi. *The Awakening of Kundalini*. New York: E.P. Dutton, 1975.

Lappe, Frances Moore. *Diet for a Small Planet*. New York: Ballantine Books, 1971.

Lasch, Christopher. *The Culture of Narcissism*. New York: W.W. Norton, 1979.

Le Shan, Lawrence. *How to Meditate*. New York: Bantam, 1975.

Levine, Steven. *Gradual Awakening*. New York: Doubleday, 1989.

Ludeman, Kay, and Henderson, Louise. *Resource Handbook on Allergies*. Dallas: Ludeman & Henderson, 1978.

Masters, R.E., and Houston, J. *Varieties of Psychedelic Experience*. New York: Holt, Rinehart, & Winston, 1966.

McCartney, James. *Yoga, the Key to Life*. New York: E.P. Dutton, 1969.

Moody, Raymond A., Jr., M.D. *Life after Life*. New York: Harper & Row, 1976.

Ornstein, Robert E., ed. *The Nature of Human Consciousness*. San Francisco: W.H. Freeman, 1973.

Pelletier, Kenneth R. *Toward a Science of Consciousness*. Berkeley, Ca.: Celestial Arts, 1988.

Pelletier, Kenneth R. *A New Age: Problems & Potential*. San Francisco: Robert Briggs Associates, 1985.

Pelletier, Kenneth R. *Mind as Healer, Mind as Slayer: A Holistic Approach to Preventing Stress Disorders.* New York: Dell, 1977.

Rajneesh, Bhagwan Shree. *Only One Sky.* New York: E.P. Dutton, 1975.

Reinhold, H.A., ed. *The Soul Afire: Revelations of the Mystics.* Meridian Books, 1944.

Robertson, Laurel, Flinders, Carol, and Godfrey, Bronwen. *Laurel's Kitchen: A Handbook for Vegetarian Cookery and Nutrition.* Berkeley, Ca.: Nilgiri Press, 1976.

Roszak, Theodore. *The Cult of Information.* New York: Pantheon, 1986.

Schwarz, Jack. *Human Energy Systems.* New York: E.P. Dutton, 1979.

Schwarz, Jack. *Voluntary Controls.* New York: E.P. Dutton, 1978.

Schwarz, Jack. *The Path of Action.* New York: E.P. Dutton, 1977.

Smith, Huston. *Forgotten Truth: The Primordial Tradition.* New York: Harper & Row, 1976.

Suzuki-roshi, Shunryu. *Zen Mind, Beginner's Mind.* New York: Weatherhill, 1970.

Thich Nhat Hanh. *The Miracle of Mindfulness.* Berkeley, Ca.: Parallax Press.

Thomas, Anna. *The Vegetarian Epicure.* New York: Vintage Books, 1972.

Trungpa, Chogyam. *Glimpses of Abhidharma.* Boulder, Co.: Prajna Press, 1978.

Trungpa, Chogyam. *Meditation in Action.* Berkeley, Ca.: Shambhala Publications, Inc., 1970.

Tulku Tarthang (Ed.). *Reflections of Mind.* Berkeley, Ca.: Dharma Publishing Co., 1975.

Watts, Alan W. *The Way of Zen.* New York: Vintage Books.

Weil, Andrew. *The Natural Mind: A New Way of Looking at Drugs and the Higher Consciousness.* Boston, Ma.: Houghton Mifflin, 1972.

Wilson, Colin. *Access to Inner Worlds.* Berkeley, Ca.: Celestial Arts, 1990.

Wilson, Colin. *Mysteries.* New York: G.P. Putnam & Sons, 1979.

Yogonanda, Paramahansa. *The Science of Religion.* California: Self-Realization Fellowship, 1953.

Young, Arthur M. *The Reflexive Universe.* San Francisco: Robert Briggs Associates, 1985.